TEA SOMMELIER

...THERE CAME A KNOCK AT THE DOOR, AND THE BUTLER ENTERED
WITH A LADEN TEA-TRAY AND SET IT DOWN UPON A SMALL JAPANESE
TABLE. THERE WAS A RATTLE OF CUPS AND SAUCERS AND THE HISSING
OF A FLUTED GEORGIAN URN. TWO GLOBE-SHAPED CHINA DISHES
WERE BROUGHT IN BY A PAGE. DORIAN GRAY WENT OVER
AND POURED OUT THE TEA.

Oscar Wilde

from The Picture of Dorian Gray

WHITE STAR PUBLISHERS

Project editor VALERIA MANFERTO DE FABIANIS

Editorial assistant LAURA ACCOMAZZO

Graphic layout CLARA ZANOTTI

4

PHOTOS BY FABIO PETRONI

TEXTS BY GABRIELLA LOMBARDI

RECIPES BY CHEF GIOVANNI RUGGIERI

CONTENTS

FOREWORD

Before becoming a tea lover, I was a big coffee drinker who snubbed all forms of tea, whether served in cafes or prepared at home. Then I discovered pure tea leaves, and that was a sheer revelation.

I have fallen hopelessly in love with this drink and its rituals, first and foremost for its ever changing fragrances. These I can savor every time I visit a production area, or simply taste the latest crops, which are never the same as the previous. I love the feeling of being able to understand the spirit of a place from the first few sips, and the atmosphere of hospitality and conviviality that is created around a cup of tea, encouraging people to stop for a moment, for a chat and to share their thoughts.

Tea takes you on a voyage of discovery of the rites and cultures of distant lands, and a lifetime is simply not enough to become fully conversant with this extraordinary drink.

Travelling abroad, I realized that tea is actually very much in fashion, despite being considered quite passé in Italy. The desire to spread the word on its contemporary allure has been quickened by the encounter with two professionals, with whom I share a common vision. The result is this book, the pure and sharp aesthetics of which, expressed through beautiful images and haute cuisine dishes, exquisitely matches my interpretation of the tea universe.

Many words have been spent to describe the multi-faceted world of tea. The main aim of this work is to clarify the many inaccuracies and conflicting information revolving around tea, starting with its complex jargon. The objective, therefore, is to provide simple and intuitive, yet accurate and precise information on tea, while also arousing the curiosity and interest of anyone wishing to approach pure teas: enthusiasts, connoisseurs, industry insiders and, why not, a good many novices.

After a brief history, we will discuss the botanical and chemical aspects of tea, as well as its health properties, followed by a description of various preparation techniques and the ideal accessories required in each case. Even the best tea, when prepared incorrectly, will not achieve its full potential, which is why we have focused on traditional, tried and true preparations. Although it is true that taste is subjective, the correct method of preparation can be learned, and constitutes the essential standard on which to base the criteria for evaluating tea quality.

Each tea family offers products of excellence. These pages are an invitation to discover the best crus that everyone should taste, at least once in their life.

As the tea ritual is all about pleasure, you will also find the best foods to be served with each variety, as well as delicious recipes based on tea leaves, extending the delights of this drink from the cup to the dish.

Finally, I confess that I have written this book in the hope that people will stop telling me: "I don't like tea." I am convinced that there is the right tea for everyone, capable of opening up a new world of sensations. I invite you to find the right tea for you... the one that you too will fall in love with.

THE ORIGINS OF TEA

The history of tea is an ancient one, and indeed there are legends in every country surrounding its origins. Perhaps the most famous is the Chinese story of the Emperor Shen Nong, the father of agriculture and medicine, who was very strict about hygiene and only drank boiling water. One day, in the year 2737 BC, he was boiling some water when leaves from a nearby tea shrub blew into the cauldron, giving the water a golden hue. Intrigued, the emperor exclaimed: "That which Heaven sends, brings harmony into our soul." He tasted the resulting brew, and the beverage of tea was born. For the Indians, tea was discovered by Bodhidharma, son of Kosjuwo, King of the Indies. Prince Bodhidharma, who had converted to Buddhism, went to China to spread the word. Having vowed not to sleep for seven years of meditation, after the first five years he was overcome by fatigue, and took to chewing leaves from a shrub, which acted as a stimulant, helping him stay awake. These were, of course, tea leaves. According to Japanese Buddhists, instead, after three years of waking, Bodhidharma fell asleep and dreamt of the women he had loved in his youth. Upon waking, he cut off his own eyelids in disgust at himself. He threw the eyelids away, and from them sprouted a wild shrub whose leaves produce an extraordinary drink capable of giving strength and helping to stay awake during long meditation.

Setting legends aside, tea is one of the major Chinese contributions to humanity and civilization. China is without doubt the tea plant's country of origin, and the Chinese people the first to discover and use it. Over the centuries, the custom of drinking tea has given rise to an industry of vast proportions and to a refined and varied culture spread across the globe. The history of tea is long and complex, and would deserve a treatise of its own. Here we will limit ourselves to a brief overview, following the major stages of the dissemination and use of tea in China

ANCIENT TIMES AND THE EARLIEST DYNASTIES: THE DAWNING OF TEA

Tea has been consumed in China since time immemorial. The leaves of the tea plant, native to the area bordering with China, Laos and Myanmar, were already used as a bitter medicinal herb between the eleventh and the eighth century BC, as revealed in early sources, in which the ancient word "tu" is used to denote the tea plant as a healing remedy. The Chinese consider the area of Xishuangbanna, in Yunnan, the birthplace of tea, and here many wild tea plants can still be found to this day. The first plantations were established in the fourth century AD, in Yunnan and Sichuan. Originally, tea was only consumed as a beverage in the ancient Ba-Shu, in southwest China. When trade and cultural exchanges intensified, the practice of drinking tea spread along the Yangtze River and in the Central Plains. Tea culture made its first shy appearance during the Wei and Jin dynasties and the Southern and Northern Dynasties, when economic and cultural exchanges and the unification of north and south spread consumption further north. During the ancient Han Dynasty (206 BC - 220 AD), the provinces of Changsha, Hunan and Chaling became tea production hubs.

THE TANG DYNASTY: BIRTH OF THE TEA CULTURE

The powerful Tang dynasty (618-907) boasted a strong economy and a flourishing culture. According to historians, tea, now part of everyday life, became fashionable at this time and further prospered under the Song dynasty. Indeed, during the Tang dynasty, tea also became popular in the north of the country. The reasons are to be found in the birth and spread of the Chan Buddhist sect. The followers of this sect had to refrain from eating and sleeping at night, but were allowed to drink tea. As the sect's following increased, the practice became a habit. Another reason why the tea culture began to flourish during this period was the custom of offering tea as a tribute to the emperor. This period saw the publication of the first book dedicated to this drink, the renowned The Classic of Tea by Lu Yu, which was a landmark event in the establishment of the tea culture.

Venerated as the god of tea, Lu Yu (733-804) provided a broad overview of the origins, history, production, processing, infusion and tasting of tea, based on the teachings of his predecessors and the extensive research to which he devoted his life. His first monograph raised tea tasting to an art form.

Many tea varieties existed at this time. Mainly produced in round "cakes," the drink was generally prepared though boiling. Moreover, attractive preparation and serving sets began to make their appearance at the Tang imperial court.

In 641, Princess Wencheng brought tea to Tibet as part of her dowry. From that moment on, tea began to be sold in large quantities on the border with China, and was introduced in the north east and south east as a valuable asset. Tea started to be traded in exchange for horses, a practice that lasted for over a thousand years, through the Tang, Song, Ming and Qing dynasties. The Tibetans, who lived on a high plain feeding primarily on butter, beef and mutton, willingly bought tea to aid digestion and keep warm. Tibet did not produce tea, which instead was plentiful in the Chinese plains; here, on the other hand, horses were scarce. The ancient Tea-Horse Road saw the continuous transportation of mules, horses, furs and medicinal products from Tibet, Sichuan and Yunnan on the one side, and products from the Chinese plains, such as tea, clothes, salt and everyday items, on the other.

THE SONG DYNASTY: THE HEIGHT OF THE TEA CULTURE

The Song dynasty (960-1279) introduced a highly developed tea culture, tending towards refinement and luxury. During this time, greater importance was given to civil rather than military affairs. Consequently, a refined intellectual class blossomed, which produced several works of literature on the tea ritual. Emperor Hui Zong, born Zhao Ji (1082-1135), wrote the famous Treatise on Tea (Da Guan Cha Lu), the most detailed and authoritative description of the sophisticated tea ceremony in vogue during the Song Dynasty.

Furthermore, the method for preparing tea evolved from boiling, typical of the Tang dynasty, to infusion, a technique that involves both artistic and technical skills. Tea powder was placed in a bowl, boiling water was poured on top, and a special "brush" was used to stir.

Song tea was characterized by round bundles known as dragon and phoenix tea cakes. Production of these cakes evolved on such a wide scale that as many as 4000 varieties developed.

Another distinctive feature of the time was given by competitions in the art of tea preparation and serving, which became universally popular among aristocrats, scholars and ordinary people alike. The popularity of these competitions triggered an intense production of tea pottery, such as the black glazed cups typically used during the preparation rite.

Tea houses flourished during this period. Tea had become both an economically and culturally prosperous product, and an important part of everyday life. Some tea houses traded in dresses and paintings, in addition to offering the precious drink, and were decorated with flowers and paintings by famous artists. During the Southern Song dynasty, the Japanese monks Enni Bern'en and Nanpo Jomin studied Buddhism in Zhejiang, respectively in 1235 and 1259. Upon returning home, they brought back tea seeds and the dictates of tea serving.

Eisai, a prominent Japanese monk, also went to China to study the Buddhist scriptures, once in 1169 and then again in 1187, and he too returned to his motherland with seeds and the art of tea making. He later wrote a book called *Kicha Yojoki* (How to Stay Healthy by Drinking Tea), the first ever Japanese book on tea. To this day, the Japanese tea ceremony, Cha No Yu, is based on the tea powder and brush technique in vogue at the time of the Song Dynasty.

THE MING DYNASTY: TEA CULTURE, AND THE RETURN TO SIMPLICITY

During the Ming dynasty (1368-1644), the art of tasting tea underwent substantial changes. The practice in use during the Tang and Song dynasties of boiling or infusing tea powder was replaced by the infusion of tea leaves in boiling water. In 1391, Emperor Zhu Yuanzhang issued an edict according to which loose tea could be offered in tribute instead of tea cakes. This was because loose tea was becoming appreciated for its simplicity and for the way it preserved the natural flavor of tea. Tea competitions fell out of fashion, and as powdered leaves were no longer in use, accessories such as metal or stone mortars, stoves and brushes, were abandoned in favor of terracotta and porcelain teapots. A particularly fine and permeable clay, rich in iron, was discovered roughly midway through the Ming dynasty in Fixing, in the Jiangsu province. Since then, the best teapots are made with this clay, which helps to enhance the natural flavor of tea.

During the Ming dynasty, monarchical absolutism and centralization of power reached their peak, making it impossible for many intellectuals and artists to express their talent. As a result, they turned to other activities, such as travelling, music, chess, painting and calligraphy, all practices that coexist harmoniously with tea drinking. Many tea experts in the Ming dynasty were, in fact, eminent scholars, who wrote more than fifty books on tea, many of which have been handed down from generation to generation.

THE QING DYNASTY: THE POPULAR DIMENSION OF TEA

During the early phase of the Qing dynasty (1644-1911), tea spread throughout the world. Chinese tea exports increased rapidly, reaching a record production of 134 million kilograms (301.5million kilograms) in 1886. Chinese tea had monopolized the world market, although shortly afterwards exports experienced a significant drop as China lost its overseas markets in India, Sri Lanka, Indonesia and Japan, where local cultivations had taken root. During the Qing dynasty, the Chinese tea culture became a part of family life. Gradually, the Chinese tea ceremony also became widespread in the Western world.

There was a great proliferation of tea houses, and the habit of drinking tea became extremely popular. Both in rural and urban areas, public tea houses became pivotal to the everyday life of Chinese subjects, and fulfilled the function of meeting and entertainment centers. This led to the development of an extraordinary and diverse tea house culture.

Many specialized shops also began to crop up.

The early twentieth century saw a significant boost in the tea industry in the regions of Jiangxi, Anhui and Zhejiang, where new tea cultivation and processing techniques were designed and developed.

In 1940, the Agricultural College of Fudan University, in Shanghai, set up a department for tea studies, and the first specialized tea training course.

THE DISSEMINATION OF TEA IN EUROPE

It is unclear whether tea was first introduced in Europe by the Portuguese or the Dutch. The Portuguese were the first to taste the drink, but they depended financially on the Dutch, who were the main importers of goods from the East.

Initially, tea was loaded into the holds of Dutch ships to fill in any space left over by other goods. It wasn't until 1637 that the Dutch East India Company sensed its profit potential. The Dutch soon became aficionados of the drink. Gradually, tea began to take hold in Germany and France. News about the Eastern drink and its health benefits also reached England, where it was warmly greeted.

Tea had already been in use in Russia since 1567, imported from China via caravan routes, and indeed the country had developed an original method for its preparation through the use of the samovar.

It wasn't until the mid 1600s that tea reached America, when the Dutch founded New Amsterdam, or present day New York.

Tea is thought to have reached Italy at the hands of the Bersaglieri veterans of the Crimean War in 1855.

THE TEA PLANT

BOTANICS, VARIETIES, CULTIVATION, HARVESTS,
AND DIFFUSION

A century later, Robert Fortune discovered that all teas derive from a single plant: an evergreen shrub called Camellia sinensis (L.) O. Kuntze.

We are used to thinking of the tea plant as a shrub. However, if it is not pruned it can grow as tall as around 33-49 feet (10-15 meters). In Yunnan, there are many age-old tea trees, the oldest dating back 2700-3200 years.

Ancient Chinese history records reveal that the leaves of the wild tea plant were first used for medical purposes, and that the first plantations, in Yunnan and Sichuan, were established in the fourth century AD. From then on, the plant was "tamed," transforming it from a tall tree into a shrub, for ease of harvesting.

The pruned plant takes the form of a bush-shaped woody shrub. This optimizes the crown, thus maximizing the number of leaves available.

Indeed, by pruning the top buds, the plant grows outwards rather than upwards.

The leaf tea is simple, symmetrical, either oval or lance-shaped, with serrated edges and a midrib.

The tea plant reproduces through seeds or cuttings. In the past, the plants were grown naturally from seeds, but nowadays cuttings are preferred. A cutting has an identical DNA to that of the parent plant. Every seed, on the other hand, is different from the next, and therefore every new plant will have a different genetic makeup to that of the parent plant. When a parent plant – i.e. a plant that grows directly from seed – produces a top-rate tea, it is used to create cuttings.

Cloning plants that resist certain climatic conditions and pest attacks, or simply the most productive or those that produce high quality teas, guarantees consistent levels of production.

Tea cuttings are shoots of a parent plant that are removed and placed in soil until the roots sprout. When the new plants have reached a height of around 8 inches (15-20 cm), they are ready to be planted.

In southern China, as we have seen, the tea plant has grown naturally since ancient times, thanks to favorable weather conditions. The natural environment surrounding young tea plants profoundly influences their quality. The flavor of tea will vary by changing just one of the fundamental elements, such as soil, water, climate and sun exposure. The plants that grow in tropical and subtropical regions marked by a mild climate, and the optimal proportion of humidity, rain and sun, produce the highest quality teas. The tea plant requires a well-drained acidic soil and a rainy, cloudy, foggy and mildly sunny climate.

The best teas are produced in the mountains, where the plantations enjoy the best conditions in which to grow. These teas are appreciated for their freshness and their lingering aromatic notes, suitable for multiple infusions. For plain-growing teas, it is important to shade the plants, creating the optimal undergrowth conditions for their growth.

Tea quality also depends on the harvest season. Spring is by far the best. At this time, the buds are dark green, smooth, full-bodied, and with a good water content, and are rich in aromas and highly antioxidant and nutritional substances.

There are hundreds of botanical specimens of Camellia Sinensis. Indeed, a Chinese proverb says that we can count the stars in the sky, but we cannot give a name to every tea.

These specimens are classified in several ways, in addition to the six macro-families split by color classification (green, white, yellow, blue-green, red and black). For example, they can be classified by harvest season into spring, summer and autumn teas. They can be defined mountain or plain teas, depending on where they were cultivated.

Moreover, harvesting may be manual or mechanical, although a manual harvest enables the selection of the best shoots and leaves.

The tea plant, like other tropical plants, alternates stages of growth and rest. Shoots sprout during the growth stages, and these are carefully harvested and processed. Unlike for other intensive farming crops, only the leaves of the tea plant are picked, ignoring fruits, flowers or seeds. In Japan, tea is harvested four times a year. The warmer and more constant climate of Africa, instead, permits continuous harvesting throughout the year.

There are various types of harvesting methods, chosen by the producer, and these determine the quality of the end product:

- just the shoot
- the shoot and one leaf
- the shoot and two leaves
- the shoot and three leaves
- the shoot and four leaves
- the shoot and five leaves

Mechanical or semi-mechanical harvesting is widespread in countries where the cost of labor is too high (in Japan, for example) or where standard or poor quality tea reserved for tea bags is produced on a large scale (the "crush, tear and curl" method practiced mainly in India).

THE CHEMISTRY OF TEA

Depending on the chemical reaction undergone by the leaves during processing, tea is classified as:

- non-oxidized (green tea)
- oxidized (white, yellow, blue-green and red tea)
- fermented (black Chinese teas and Pu'er teas)

Oxidation is a chemical reaction that takes place through the presence of oxygen. Fermentation, unlike oxidation, takes place through the presence of yeasts and bacteria on the tea leaves.

Tea contains:

- catechins (green tea is high in ECGC, powerful anti-oxidants that fight the free radicals responsible for ageing and some degenerative diseases);
- oxidized polyphenols (the theaflavins and thearubigins present in fully oxidized teas; these perform a lower protective action than catechins);
- alkaloids (caffeine, theobromine and theophylline, substances that alter brain function, improve concentration and digestion, and have diuretic and vasodilatory properties; caffeine releases more slowly in tea than in coffee, because in tea caffeine tends to bind to the polyphenols - which is why coffee is considered a stimulant, while tea is considered more invigorating and refreshing);
- amino acids (the protein components required for cell renewal);
- water, sugars, and important vitamins such as A, B, C, E and K;
- minerals (such as calcium, magnesium, manganese, potassium, fluorine and zinc);
- glucosides (substances that give rise to essential oils, providing the aromatic notes of tea).

THE HEALING PROPERTIES OF TEA

Traditional Chinese medicine recommends drinking at least 3 cups of tea a day to keep healthy.

Recent international studies, presented in New York on 19 September 2012 during the "5th International Scientific Symposium on Tea & Human Health," reveal the health-giving properties of the main substances contained in tea.

In particular, polyphenols are powerful antioxidants, fighting cell damage caused by the free radicals produced as part of normal cell metabolism or as a result of stressful events (radiation, smoke, pollution, UV rays, emotional and physical stress, chemical additives, bacterial and viral attacks, etc.).

Although tea cannot replace fruits and vegetables in the diet, science shows that its leaves contain a higher concentration of antioxidants than most products rich in these molecules. The antioxidant activity of two cups of tea is equal to seven glasses of orange juice, five medium-sized onions or four medium-sized apples.

More specifically, polyphenols:

- have anti-cancer properties; tea drinkers are less likely to develop cancer than non-tea drinkers;
- are powerful anti-inflammatories that play a preventive role against the risk of cardiovascular disease, particularly heart disease and stroke;
- neutralize free radicals due to their antioxidant properties;
- stimulate the metabolism by decreasing the absorption of fat and favoring weight management;
- lower the level of cholesterol and sugar in the blood;
- boost the immune system;
- play a role in preventing the loss of bone mass;
- decrease the general and lung damage caused by cigarette smoke;
- protect teeth against caries;
- protect the skin against damage caused by sun rays;
- have an anti-inflammatory effect on the digestive system and intestinal tract.

Caffeine and other substances that stimulate the central nervous system also have beneficial effects on the human body. In particular, they:

- stimulate concentration;
- aid digestion and diuresis.

In terms of amino acids, L-Theanine reduces stress and anxiety responses associated with premenstrual syndrome. Recent studies have shown that L-Theanine increases concentration and relaxation, and improves sleep disorders.

THE COLORS OF TEA

COLOR CLASSIFICATION OF TEA

For a long time, it was thought, especially in the West, that green and black tea came from two separate plants. In fact, there is just one tea plant, known by the name of Camellia Sinensis, while the various types of tea available stem from a number of factors, such as local climatic conditions, harvesting methods and processing techniques. In China, tea is traditionally classified into six families, based on the color taken on by the leaves and liquor after processing. According to this color classification, tea can be split into the following macro-categories:

GREEN TEAS
WHITE TEAS
YELLOW TEAS
BLUE-GREEN TEAS
RED TEAS
BLACK TEAS

Each of these categories includes a great variety of extremely different products, encompassing a world of unique sensorial experiences just waiting to be discovered.
Indeed, these six families are to be considered general categories, comparable in the West to the distinction between red, white and rosé wines.

QUALITY ASSESSMENT: TEA CLASSIFICATIONS AND TERMS

Over 3,000 types of tea are produced in the world, and these differ according to the processing method adopted.
In this book we will relate the production techniques specific to each family. As regards the classification of finished products, in this chapter we provide an overview of the assessment methods, terms and acronyms used to assess the quality of tea.
Tea is generally assessed by visually examining the appearance and color of the infusion, and by sampling its flavor, perfume and aroma.
The appearance is assessed in terms of strength or delicacy, color and brilliance, purity or impurity.
Once the tea leaves have undergone the full processing cycle and have been dried, they are classified by experts, who assess the quality of the tea based on their appearance and type.
The first significant distinction, based on the appearance of the leaves, is classified as follows: leaf quality (full leaves), broken quality (broken leaves) and fanning quality (roughly chopped leaves, generally used for tea bags).
It is important for the leaves or leaf pieces used for a particular tea variety to be of the same size. This is because, during infusion, the leaves release a different aroma, color and intensity depending on their size. The smaller the leaf, the faster the infusion time required; conversely, the bigger the leaf, the longer the infusion time.
A number of terms, designed to create an international parameter of assessment, are used for the leaf category.

FOP: *Flowery Orange Pekoe*

This indicates a tea made using the last shoot and the first leaf below it. Young, tender leaves guarantee high quality tea.

GFOP: *Golden Flowery Orange Pekoe*

FOP varieties added to with golden tips, i.e. the slender, yellow-golden tips of the shoots.

TGFOP: *Tippy Golden Flowery Orange Pekoe*

FOP varieties with a greater percentage of golden tips.

FTGFOP: *Finest Tippy Golden Flowery Orange Pekoe*

Top rate FOP varieties.

SFTGFOP: *Special Finest Tippy Golden Flowery Orange Pekoe.*

The best FOP varieties.

These acronyms can also be followed by the number 1, indicating first-rate quality: e.g. FTGFOP1.

The letter B before the inscription OP indicates broken tea.

Chopped tea leaves are indicated by the letter F (*fanning*).

Finally, leaves under 0.05 inches (1.5 mm) in size are classified as dust, and are produced using the *Crushing, Tearing and Curling method.*

The intrinsic nature of a specific tea quality is judged based on the color, perfume and flavor of the infusion. The first step is to observe the infusion, to identify the type, or "color." The subsequent stage is the olfactory assessment, to identify the type, intensity and persistence of the tea. Finally comes flavor, indentifying whether it is rich or delicate, full-bodied or thin, ripe or unripe, fresh or stale.

The leaves are first observed in their dried state, and then once infused, to assess their tenderness, color, brilliance and uniformity.

The experts then determine and quantify the value of the tea, through both their senses and a variety of technical instruments, such as saucers, cups and bowls, following a well-defined procedure described in the chapter dedicated to professional tasting.

THE ART OF TEA MAKING

A COMPARISON BETWEEN EUROPEAN AND EASTERN INFUSIONS

When talking about the art of tea making, the most common questions are: "how much," and "how long?" As we will see below, these are difficult questions to answer, because several different factors must be considered in preparing a good cup of tea.

There are two great tea making traditions worldwide: the Chinese and the Anglo-Saxon.

The basic rules of these two schools can be summarized as follows:
• Anglo-Saxon, or Western method: few tea leaves, a long infusion time, and a single infusion;
• Chinese, or Eastern method: many tea leaves, a very short infusion time, and multiple infusions.

As we will see, it is not a question of one method being better than the other, but rather of different teas whose particular characteristics are exalted by longer or shorter infusion times.

HOW TO PREPARE AND DRINK A PROPER TEA - THE MAIN FACTORS

THE IMPORTANCE OF THE WATER, WATER TEMPERATURE, INFUSION TIMES, CHOICE OF ACCESSORIES, QUANTITY OF TEA, OPTIMAL STORAGE METHOD FOR TEA

Among the secrets found in the various phases of working with the leaves lies the promise of the secret that will be able to offer you an excellent cup of tea.

However, purchasing a quality tea is essential, although not sufficient in itself, to successfully sample a good cup of this beverage. Poor preparation can ruin a good product, or simply not allow for all of the fragrances and aromas that it could possibly release to come through.

Preparing tea seems like a simple task: outwardly, it suffices to pour hot water over dry leaves, wait a few minutes, and problem solved. Often though, once the brew is in the cup, it is too dark, sour, bitter, strong or simply not pleasant to drink without adding sugar, milk, lemon, or honey to correct the problem. Before blaming the quality of tea, you can put a few simple tricks to use that can favor a better and sometimes, truly surprising, end result.

Always bearing your personal preferences and tastes in mind, once you have chosen a quality tea, do not be afraid to experiment by varying the procedure until you have achieved a fully satisfying result.

Below are what we believe to be the main factors that play a role in preparing good tea.

THE IMPORTANCE OF THE WATER

The quality of the water is just as important as the quality of the dried tea used for the infusion.

In the cup, the color and aroma of the brew depend on the type of water used during preparation.

By assessing the end result, it will be clear that good water enhances the quality of the tea, just as poor water will alter the infusion even of the best leaves.

Lu Yu, in *The Classic of Tea*, recommended using the same water that nourished the tea plant while it was growing. Even without going to such an extent, you can use mineral or spring water. What is important is that it is pure, odorless, colorless, mildly acidic (with a pH less than 7), soft (the softness or hardness of water is expressed in French degrees; in this case, to qualify as soft the water must not exceed a limit of 8° F) and with a minimal mineral content (with a dry residue < 50 mg/l).

WATER TEMPERATURE

Using a water boiler with temperature control will allow you to make the best extraction possible from your favorite tea. With the exception of hygienic reasons, the water should never boil. Water loses its oxygen content when it is boiled, and this plays a fundamental role in transferring the aromatic compounds to a gaseous state, and their being perceived as a scent. Furthermore, after boiling, the minerals in the water tend to form a film on the surface of the water which does not react well with the tea.

Controlling the temperature of the water and other basic parameters helps to avoid errors and to keep a good balance in the brew between tannins, amino acids, minerals and aromatic compounds. An excessively high temperature risks "burning" the tea, destroying the amino acids and the aromatic compounds. It will also accelerate the extraction of polyphenols, making the tea more bitter and sour. An excessively low temperature, in contrast, will prevent some teas from "blossoming," from completely allowing the leaves to unfurl. The brew will not be balanced in this case as well. Some teas with tightly rolled leaves, such as Wulong, or compressed teas, require temperatures that are just below boiling in order to soften gradually.

As a general rule, indications for water temperature are:

- 160-185° F (70-85° C) for Japanese green teas and for all other delicate, young, and freshly picked teas;
- 175-185° F (80-85° C) for green, yellow, and white teas;
- 185-195° F (85-90° C) for red teas with buds and spring Darjeeling teas;
- 185-205° F (85-95° C) for Wulong or rolled teas;
- and 195-210° F (90-98° C) for fermented, compressed, black Indian or Singhalese teas.

This is the parameter that is most likely to be highly debated.

Although it mainly depends on one's personal inclination toward a more delicate or intense taste, normally high quality teas require shorter infusion times compared to standard quality teas. Freshness also plays an important role: young and fresh spring teas or teas with a high percentage of buds require even shorter infusion times.

CHOICE OF ACCESSORIES

There is no right or wrong teapot, and it cannot be said that one of the two methods of preparation, Eastern or Western, is better than the other. However, it is correct to say that the union between certain teas and certain accessories will allow for an optimal result to be achieved, highlighting the quality of the tea. Certain types of tea, such as fermented or Wulong, express all of their potential with the Gong Fu Cha method. Often, the quality of these teas can be captured by the number of possible infusions.

Other teas, in contrast, require longer infusion times to release their aromas. For these, the Western method is superior.

QUANTITY OF TEA

As we have seen before, an absolute rule does not exist. Instead, there are two schools of thought: Eastern and Western. The first calls for short infusion times and a greater quantity of leaves. The second utilizes a smaller quantity of tea in one single infusion for a prolonged period.

For the Eastern quantity, the quantity of dried leaves adapts to a very small container such as the Yi Xing teapot or Gaiwan teacup. Using the Gong Fu Cha method, the proportion of leaves should be around a third or even half the size of the container. Considering a capacity of 2/3 of a cup (150 ml), around 1/8 oz (5-6 grams) of tea is needed.

With a Western quantity, using a container of the same size, the quantity is practically cut in half. The tea/water ratio is in the order of 1/5 to 1/7, so you need to calculate around 1/16 oz (2-3 g) for each 2/3 of a cup (150 ml).

THE ART OF TEA MAKING 茶

Choosing the right accessories enhances the tea's flavour, colour and scent.

OPTIMAL STORAGE METHOD FOR TEA

Tea's enemies are light, moisture, and odors. To maintain the freshness and aromas of a quality tea, you should follow a few simple storage rules. First of all, never store tea in a glass or transparent container. And above all, never buy it from someone who stores it like this. A quality tea stored in an incorrect manner will lose its organoleptic properties. You should always choose containers that are airtight and opaque.

Tea leaves are very porous and they absorb moistures and odors in their environment. Tea containers must be placed in cool environments that are well ventilated and far from spices, coffee, cheese, or other foods with strong odors.

Grand cru teas must be consumed within one year from when they are picked.

THE ART OF TEA MAKING

THE RUSSIAN ART OF TEA MAKING: THE SAMOVAR

The Samovar and its use are typical and compelling expressions of Russian culture. Since the nineteenth century, when the culture of tea spread across the Russian provinces, the samovar has been considered the hearth of every home, and the very symbol of hospitality.

This item, with its unusual appearance and function, is a kind of kettle that keeps water constantly at the right temperature. Once the water was heated over a brazier, but today samovars are electric and usually made of steel, although other possible materials include silver, gold and porcelain. On top of the hot water boiler is a recess in which the teapot is placed.

- Russian tea is prepared with highly concentrated, strong dark tea, in the proportion of half water and half tea leaves.
- Once the tea is filtered, the teapot is placed on top of the samovar, where the concentrated tea remains warm due to the water vapor emanating from the boiler.
- Whenever someone wants a cup of tea, approx. 0.4-0.8 inches (1-2 cm) of concentrated tea is poured into a cup and this is diluted by adding hot water from the samovar's tap.
- The tea is served with jam, blinis, milk, orange peel, candied fruit and sugar cubes. The latter are held between the teeth, to sweeten the tea as it passes from the cup into the mouth.

THE ART OF TEA MAKING

THE MOROCCAN ART OF TEA MAKING: MINT TEA

Mint and wormwood infusions are traditional in North Africa, where tea drinking was introduced as late as the mid-nineteenth century by the British. At this time, the Crimean War threatened British trade routes to Slavic countries, and so the English were forced to find new outlets in North Africa. Tea soon became a hit with the Moroccans. Local customs meant the new drink was often mixed with traditional flavors, such as mint, wormwood and sage.

Drinking green tea with mint has become a fully-fledged daily rite, celebrated during business negotiations, important moments of family life, or simply to welcome a guest.

The Chinese Gunpowder green tea, native to Zhejiang, is the variety used in Morocco and in other Arab countries for their tea ritual.

To prepare mint tea, first bring some water to the boil.

- Put two tablespoons of Gunpowder green tea in a silver or metal teapot, then pour some boiling water over the tea leaves. Rinse quickly and throw away the water.
- Add a handful of fresh Nana mint leaves and 5 to 7 cubes of white sugar.
- Stir and leave to infuse for 4-5 minutes.
- Pour the tea into a glass and then transfer it back into the pot.
- Repeat three times to mix all the ingredients well.
- Put a teaspoon of pine nuts into the empty glass.
- The tea is served with pine nuts and typical Arab desserts made with honey, coconut, walnuts, almonds and sesame seeds.

ICED TEA: PREPARATION METHODS

When you have good quality tea, it is really very simple to prepare a tasty iced tea to offer friends at a party, for an original aperitif, or simply to quench your thirst on hot summer days.

There are two methods of preparation, one hot and the other cold.

The first results in a stronger flavored, more persistent drink. Prepare the hot infusion using approx. 1/16 oz (2-3 g) of tea per 2/3 cup (150 ml) of water. The infusion time will be one minute longer than the time indicated in the preparation tables. Once filtered, the tea is poured into a shaker filled with ice cubes. To sweeten (optional), add a tablespoon of liquid brown sugar. Serve in red wine glasses, garnished with fresh fruit.

The cold infusion results in a more delicate, crystal-clear drink, almost like scented water, with no bitter after taste. If you have the time, this method is definitely the best.

Place about 1/2 oz (15-18 g) of tea in a glass jar.

Pour a liter of cool or tepid water on the leaves.

Immediately place the jar in the refrigerator, for about 4 hours for green tea and about 6 hours for Wulong, black or blended tea. It is advisable not to prepare the infusion at room temperature, as the dry leaves may contain bacteria in the form of spores. At hot or cold temperatures, the spores remain inactive, but at room temperature and in the presence of water, they may reactivate.

Before serving, filter the iced tea into large wine glasses, and garnished with fresh fruit.

THE ART OF TEA MAKING

PROFESSIONAL TEA TASTING
EQUIPMENT AND ASSESSMENT METHODS

The first comparative teas tastings and competitions were held in China as early as the 8th century AD. In the West, professional tasting took hold in the late 1800s, when tea, imported from China and India, was often adulterated, with new and old harvests blended together, or tea leaves mixed with those of other plants. This led to the need to check imported products, before allowing them to be sold, with tea companies beginning to train professional tea tasters and tea blenders.

Professional tea tasting enables the sampling and comparison of a great number of teas, creating a universal standard of assessment that can be recreated, based on set parameters.
The professional tea tasting set is made of white porcelain and comprises three pieces: a bowl-shaped cup, a small cup with a notched edge and a handle, and a lid. This set permits the preparation of small quantities of countless different teas, keeping a constant leaf/water ratio. The aim of professional tasting is to compare various samples of the same tea, deriving from different tea gardens, and to describe the quality and flaws of each. Successful tasting requires an in-depth understanding of the general characteristics of the tea being analyzed. Comparative tests will highlight any differences and similarities, and will permit the selection of the best quality teas. Wherever the tasting occurs, it is always subject to the same ISO standards and is always performed with the same equipment. The ISO standards are not a fully-fledged law, but a set of rules that determine the parameters to be followed with regard to the cups (with precise instructions on weight, diameter, curvature, height, shape, lid, etc.), the quantity of tea, the infusion time, and the water temperature. A comparative analysis between different teas can only be considered effective if all these parameters are maintained, the only variable being the type if tea to be analyzed.

Professional tea tasting is based on cups that are the natural evolution of the Gaiwan cup used in China. The method adopted is the following:
1. Place the dry tea leaves to be assessed on a saucer;
2. Lay out the tasting set, comprising of a bowl, notched cup and lid;
3. Place approx. 1/16 oz (2.8 g) of tea on the bottom of the notched cup;
4. Pour approx. 2/3 cup (140 ml) of water heated to 208° F (98° C) over the leaves, cover the cup with the lid, and leave to infuse for 6 minutes;
5. After infusion, keep the lid firmly on the notched cup and filter all the tea into the bowl;
6. The tasting can now begin, analyzing the dry leaves, the liquor (the actual tea), and the soaked leaves.

WITH REGARD TO THE DRY AND SOAKED LEAVES, THE TASTER WILL PERFORM:
- a visual analysis: shape and size of the leaves, color and brilliance, composition (e.g. shoots only, shoots with open leaves, leaves only, etc.), flaws and imperfections (e.g. broken leaves, stains, fungi, twigs, etc.);
- an olfactory analysis: aromatic notes;
- a tactile analysis: consistency, friability, elasticity and softness of the leaves..

WITH REGARD TO THE LIQUOR, THE TASTER WILL PERFORM:
- a visual analysis: shape and size of the leaves, color and brilliance, composition (e.g. shoots only, shoots with open leaves, leaves only, etc.), flaws and imperfections (e.g. broken leaves, stains, fungi, twigs, etc.);
- an olfactory analysis: aromatic notes;
- a tactile analysis: consistency, friability, elasticity and softness of the leaves.

With regard to the olfactory analysis, it is necessary to point out that sensitivity to odors is subjective, and varies from one individual to another. Recognizing odors is a question of practice: it means associating the sensations we perceive with the information and experiences embedded in our memory. Scents are pivotal to successful tea tasting. Practice in this regard permits an effective assessment of tea quality, based on the right balance between aromatic notes.

As regards the taste analysis, the following are of particular importance:
Body or texture: given by the tea's astringency, softness, smoothness, temperature, heat, freshness, etc. These tactile experiences are felt in the mouth, on the tongue, lips and palate.
Taste: given by the flavor (sweet, salty, bitter, sour, umami) and texture of the tea.
Scent: this is detected by the nose (through direct olfactory input, or inhalation); a pleasant smell is referred to as perfume, and unpleasant one as smell.
Aroma (given by the taste and scent): this is detected by the mouth (through indirect olfactory input), and is the most important phase of tea tasting.

PROFESSIONAL TEA TASTING

TEA SCENTS

Original "pure" teas have specific scents given by the type of cultivar, the climate conditions, the chemical composition of the soil, and the processing methods developed over the years. Constant studies allow us to understand the specific characteristics and notes typical of each tea.

There are macro olfactory families that correspond to the scents detected while tasting tea.

These families are not mutually exclusive, and indeed their notes can blend together beautifully.

VEGETABLE FAMILY: freshly cut grass, hay, herbs, cooked vegetables (asparagus, artichokes, spinach, zucchini), moss, mushrooms, humus, undergrowth.

FRUITY FAMILY: apples, pears, grapes, plums, peaches, apricots, tropical fruits, citrus fruits, cooked fruits (black cherry jam, plum jam), nuts (dates, walnuts, almonds, hazelnuts, chestnuts).

FLORAL FAMILY: jasmine, orchid, rose, orange blossom, peony, osmanthus, hawthorn, linden wild flowers.

AQUATIC FAMILY: seaweed, crustaceans, fish skin, mollusks.

WOODY FAMILY: green wood, dry wood, cedar, cigar, bark, sandalwood.

"CONFISERIE" FAMILY: honey, butter, cream, milk, sugar, vanilla, chocolate, caramel.

BALSAMIC FAMILY: pine, resin, incense.

SPICY FAMILY: cinnamon, pepper, nutmeg, cloves.

EMPYREUMATIC FAMILY: tobacco, cocoa, smoked, toasted, grilled.

ANIMAL FAMILY: game, fur, cat urine, wet dog, leather.

In this section we will provide a brief and concise glossary of terms used to taste and assess the quality of tea. This list claims to be neither complete nor technically accurate, partly because different cultures have developed different lexicons, and partly because, while there may be a certain amount of common terminology, especially in the English language, every tea taster and expert can contribute his or her own.

The following overview is provided as a general introduction, in order to impart some of the unusual and lively expressions connected with the world of tea.

COMMENTS ON THE APPEARANCE OF LEAVES

Body: relates to the appearance of the leaves, which can be old or tender, light or heavy, and have a thick or thin flesh. Generally speaking, tender, thick and heavy leaves are best.

Clear tip: the white down on the shoot is known as the "white tip;" if the shoot has several tips covered in thick down, these are defined as "clear tips;" the tips can be gold, silver or grey.

Dry: dry tea leaves that have not yet been steeped.

Flawed leaf: a badly cut leaf presenting rough edges on both sides of the cut.

Heaviness: rolled leaves that are perceived as heavy in the hand.

Infusion: steeped tea leaves removed from the water.

Powder: the powder produced after rolling, generally associated with low quality tea and often used in tea bags.

Shoots: tender tips, covered with white down, that have not grown into a full leaf.

Tender leaves: tea consisting mainly of shoots with one or two leaves; these are round, narrow, thin, and with sharp pointy tips.

Uneven leaves: leaves of uneven shape or thickness.

Well proportioned leaves: leaves with a uniform shape, whether big or small, long or short, heavy or light.

COMMENTS ON THE COLOR OF LEAVES

Black-brown: brownish black, with shades of grey.

Brilliant: a leaf of a bright, vivid color.

Even: a bright, homogeneous color.

Grass green: pale green, indicating old or low quality leaves, or that the enzyme activity has not been successfully blocked.

Green-black: a well-proportioned, velvety and even green, with shades of black.

Rich green: shiny jade green.

Matt: typical color of old, lusterless leaves.

Mixed: leaves of an uneven color.

Rust: dark matt red.

COMMENTS ON THE SCENT

Aroma: the overall scent perceived indirectly in the mouth.

Bouquet: the set of fragrances perceived in the nose.

Burnt: the smell of burning caused by blocked enzyme activity or inappropriate heating or drying.

Delicate aroma: elegant aroma in which no blend is perceived.

Elegant aroma: graceful and elegant floral aroma, in which no one particular flower can be detected.

Grass aroma: the scent of grass and leaves.

Pure and semi-sweet: a pure, balanced aroma.

Sweet aroma: aroma, similar to honey or syrup, reminiscent of lychees.

Toasted rice aroma: similar to the smell of popcorn, typical of lightly toasted teas.

Vegetable aroma: similar to the smell of freshly boiled cabbage; this term is often used to describe green tea.

COMMENTS ON THE COLOR OF THE LIQUOR

Brilliant: clear, shiny liquid.

Brilliant green: rich green with shades of yellow; clear and bright, this is the color of top quality green tea.

Cloudy: unclear liquor with suspended substances.

Golden: mainly yellow with shades of orange; light and brilliant, just like gold.

Green-yellow: green with a hint of yellow.

Light yellow: yellow and clear.

Liquor: in technical jargon, this is the liquid you drink, namely the tea itself.

Orange: yellow with a hint of red, just like the color of ripe oranges.

Orange-red: dark yellow with shades of red.

Red: overheated or old liquor, light or dark red in color.

Yellow-green: yellow with a hint of green.

COMMENTS ON THE TASTE OF THE LIQUOR

Astringent: dries the mouth due to non-oxidized polyphenols (typical of green tea) reacting with the proteins in the saliva.

Bitter: an intense, bitter and sour aroma, that dulls the taste buds slightly.

Brisk: a strong, invigorating and refreshing flavor.

Crude and sour: an unripe, strong, sour flavor, usually due to insufficient withering.

Crude and tasteless: insipid, tending towards bitter.

Fresh: fresh and delicious, used to indicate slightly acidic tea that leaves a feeling of freshness in the mouth.

Full-bodied: A strong, full-flavored infusion.

Generous: ripe and dense; rich in flavor, without being cloyingly sweet.

Grassy and sour: a strong, sour grassy taste.

Malty: a flavor reminiscent of malt; this is an indication of good quality tea.

Metallic: the unpleasant taste typical of badly withered tea.

Persistent: leaves a lingering flavor in the mouth.

Pungent: astringent without being bitter.

Pure and delicate: ripe but not too dense.

Refined: a subtle, sophisticated taste and aroma.

Rounded: that fills the mouth with a feeling of fullness.

Semi-sweet: a sweet but balanced aroma.

Smoked: tea dried on smoky flames, providing a smoky aroma.

Strong: a full, highly astringent taste, typical of a dark liquor.

Subtle: a flavor marked by delicate yet complex aromas.

Sweet: slightly sugary, not astringent.

Tannic: the flavor of liquors rich in tannins, or polyphenols.

Tasteless or flat: the thin, bodiless taste of humid tea.

Umami: one of the five basic flavors perceived by the taste buds (the others are "sweet," "salty," "bitter" and "sour"); it is mostly used in Asian cuisine to describe the taste of glutamates, which can be detected in certain Japanese green teas.

Velvety: a harmonious flavor reminiscent of the softness of silk and velvet.

Watery: thin tea due to insufficient or inadequate infusion.

GREEN TEA - CHINA

This is the most popular tea in the East. China is the world's largest producer of green tea, and can without doubt claim to offer the greatest variety. Green tea accounts for about 75% of the tea produced in China. The remaining 25% is mainly shared out among the other tea "colors:" red, fermented black and Wulong. White and yellow teas are "niche" products, accounting for minimal percentages.

The world renowned Chinese green teas are traditionally grown in Anhui, Zhejiang and Fujian. The Anhui region produces highly famed teas, such as Lu Mu Dan, Huang Shan Mao Feng, Huo Shan Huang Ya, Liu An Gua Pian, and Tai Ping Hou Kui, to name just a few. The Zhejiang region, home to the precious Long Jing, also mass produces Gunpowder, a tea of often mediocre quality, exported across the globe. The area around Fuzhou, in the Fujian region, boasts the highest production of Jasmine green tea.

Other products of excellence come from the Yunnan mountains and from the province of Jiangsu, whose Bi Luo Chun is second only to the famous Long Jing.

Green tea is the only family of teas whose leaves are not processed in such a way as to alter their chemical properties, thus preserving more than 85% of their polyphenol content and their natural green color.

The freshly picked leaves are scattered on bamboo racks and left to dry. Subsequently, depending on the method adopted, they are subjected to dry heat (in special concave containers similar to woks), air or steam. The high temperature reached blocks enzyme activity and hence the natural oxidation process, allowing the tea leaves to maintain their green color. This is the most important step in the processing of quality green tea, and releases the sweet floral, chestnut and walnut fragrance typical of green teas.

The subsequent steps differ greatly depending on the product desired. The leaves can be rolled to give them the most varied forms: twisted into spirals, folded, crushed, or rolled tightly into small pearls.

The final drying phase further reduces the residual moisture contained in the leaves. The green tea is now ready to be packaged and distributed to the market.

HOW TO PREPARE CHINESE GREEN TEA

Green tea does not require the leaves to be briefly rinsed, for which reason the infusion can be done directly in a tall and narrow glass cup in order to be able to appreciate the slow movement of the leaves which appear to dance, suspended in the water. However, according to experts, the Gaiwan cup is the best method to prepare more refined and delicate teas. It is composed of three parts: the cup, lid, and saucer. The lid serves to hold the leaves in, whether it is used as a cup or as a teapot for multiple infusions. It can be made out of different materials, but for green teas glass or porcelain is recommended.

GREEN TEA

HOW TO USE A GAIWAN TEACUP

When the Gaiwan cup is used as a teapot, we recommend that you proceed as follows:

1. Place the Gaiwan cup, jar, and glasses on the ceremonial table.
2. After bringing the water to the desired temperature, pour the hot water into the Gaiwan to heat and rinse it.
3. Discard the water and add the desired quantity of tea leaves into the Gaiwan (around 1/4 or 1/3 the volume of the Gaiwan).
4. Pour the water into the Gaiwan, and once it is filled, place the lid on it and wait;
5. Pour the tea directly into the cups or stop the infusion by pouring the brew into the jar.

During this step, you can use the strainer to prevent the leaves from being poured into the cups. With the Gaiwan cup, the infusion can be repeated several times, varying the time from 20 to 40 seconds according to personal taste. From one preparation to another, it is interesting to smell the inner portion of the lid to see how the aromas are released and develop over the course of multiple infusions.

A BIT OF ETIQUETTE FOR TEA DRINKING IF YOU GO TO CHINA

In China, when tea is served to you it is good manners to bring the index and middle fingers of the right hand together, slightly bend them and tap the table two times, symbolizing a small bow. This small ceremony, performed to show appreciation and gratitude toward the host, dates back to the Qing dynasty when Qianlong was Emperor.

During one journey to the south, the Emperor disguised himself as a servant. Once he had reached a tea house, the owner, thinking that he was a servant, gave him a teapot and ordered him to serve tea to the eunuch who had accompanied him on his journey. The eunuch, embarrassed, could not bow to his lord lest he reveal his identity, and so put his two fingers together to form a bow out of respect. Over time, this gesture of thanks spread among the common people until it became a pleasant courtesy exchanged among friends.

ANJI BAI CHA

TYPE: GREEN TEA

AREA OF PROVENANCE: CHINA, ZHEJIANG, ANJI

Anji Bai Cha tea takes its name from the village of Anji in the mountain ranges of Mu Tian, where the plantations for this wonderful green tea are to be found.

The uncontaminated surroundings, with their bamboo forests, clouds, rain and fertile soil, make this location perfect for growing a very unique tea.

In Chinese, "Bai" means white, and for this reason it is also known as Anji White Tea despite being a green tea. The "white" comes from the shoots, which are this color before they are processed. An ancient Chinese book relates of a tea plant with pale white leaves similar to jade. This story was considered a legend until the 1980s, when a tea plant with white shoots was found near Anji, which experts maintain is the plant mentioned in the book. Anji Bai Cha is produced from the leaves of this particular botanical specimen. The leaves are harvested at the beginning of spring, before the rising temperature turns them green.

The tea is rich in amino acids, with almost twice the amount of other green teas, and has calming, stress-reducing properties.

TASTING NOTES

Dry: shoots hand-worked to form flat, thin blades.

Liquor: pale yellow, crystal clear; the taste is pleasantly delicate, lingering and refreshing with the slightest hint of orchid.

Infusion: the young shoots are light green, tending to white; the harvesting method provides one shoot and one leaf.

PREPARATION

Western method: approx. 1/16 oz (2-3 grams) for every 2/3 cup (150 ml) of water at 175° F (80° C) for 2 minutes.

Eastern method: 1/8 oz (5 grams) for every 2/3 cup (150 milliliters) of water at 175° F (80° C) for up to 3 infusions of 20-30 seconds each.

Recommended with: lightly salted foods, white meats, vegetables and fish.

JADE COLUMN - YU ZHU

TYPE: GREEN TEA

AREA OF PROVENANCE: CHINA, YUNNAN, PU'ER

This tea from the plantations in the region of Pu'er (Yunnan) has a very special shape which inspired its name. It consists of a single shoot that is lovingly processed to resemble a jade colored column.

It is absolutely unique, as are all the green teas from the Yunnan mountains, and is obtained by selecting the best shoots from the spring harvest. In the cup, it expresses all the age-old culture and art of Yunnan tea. It represents sips of real poetry to be reserved for great occasions.

TASTING NOTES

Dry: a single rolled light green shoot with shades of silver.

Liquor: in the cup it is clear ivory in color; it is soft and lingering and offers a delicate flowery aroma with base notes of dried fruit (walnut) and fresh fruit (peach).

Infusion: perfectly intact and regular yellow-green leaves.

PREPARATION

Eastern method: 1/8 oz (5 grams) for every 2/3 cup (150 milliliters) of water at 175° F (80° C) for 3-5 infusions of 20-30 seconds each.

Recommended with: lightly salted foods, rice, vegetables, poultry and pork.

GREEN TEA

DONG TING BI LUO CHUN

TYPE: GREEN TEA

AREA OF PROVENANCE: CHINA, JIANGSU, DONG TING

This age-old Chinese tea is second only in fame to the Xi Hu Long Jing. The tea was created in the Temple of Ling Yuan Bi Luo Peak (Shandong), and was originally called Xia Si Xiang Ren (amazing fragrance). The Emperor Qing called it Bi Luo Chun and had it elevated to Imperial status.

Dong Ting Bi Luo Chun, produced in its area of origin, is processed entirely by hand, and only the shoots and first leaves are harvested. To give some idea of its delicacy, it is reckoned that at least 120,000 leaves are needed to produce one kilo of Bi Luo Chun First Grade.

TASTING NOTES

Dry: the light green tender leaves are a little curly; the shoots are covered with a silvery down.

Liquor: brilliant yellow; a very refreshing tea characterized by soft flowery notes.

Infusion: the steeped leaves take on a brilliant green hue; the flower notes linger and mix with those of nuts (chestnuts).

PREPARATION

Western method: approx. 1/16 oz (2-3 grams) for every 2/3 cup (150 milliliters) of water at 165-175° F (75-80° C) for 2-3 minute infusion.

Eastern method: 1/8 oz (5 grams) for every 2/3 cup (150 milliliters) of water at 165-175° F (75-80° C) for up to 3-4 infusions of 20-40 seconds each.

Recommended with: rice, fish, poultry, pork, vegetables and spicy foods.

HUANG SHAN MAO FENG

TYPE: GREEN TEA

AREA OF PROVENANCE: CHINA, ANHUI, SHE XIAN, HUANG SHAN MOUNTAINS

An old Chinese saying states that teas from the mountains are the best. The Huang Shan mountains are the best known in China for Grand Cru teas, the most famous of which must include Huang Shan Mao Feng. This historical tea sits high among the top ten most popular green teas. In the cup, the liquor appears light and brilliant, while in the mouth the aroma is intense and refreshing, with a sweet after taste.

TASTING NOTES

Dry: the tea consists of tender shoots covered with a delicate white down and with slightly curved leaves close to the buds; their shape is reminiscent of orchid buds.

Liquor: brilliant, clear gold color; the aroma is intense and intoxicating with a sweet, lingering after taste; there is perfect harmony between the flowery (orchid, magnolia), ripe fruit (apricot, mango) and chestnut notes.

Infusion: the young green-yellow shoots are tender, with a scent of nuts.

PREPARATION

Western method: approx. 1/16 oz (2-3 grams) for every 2/3 cup (150 milliliters) of water at 175° F (80° C) for 3 minute infusion.

Eastern method: 1/8 oz (5 grams) for every 2/3 cup (150 milliliters) of water at 175° F (80° C) for 3-5 infusions of 20-30 seconds each.

Recommended with: lightly salted foods, spicy foods, flavored cheeses, grilled fish, fruit, and hazelnut pie.

GREEN TEA

茶

GREEN TEA

HUO SHAN HUANG YA

TYPE: GREEN TEA

AREA OF PROVENANCE: CHINA, ANHUI, HUO SHAN

Although often sold in the west as rare yellow tea, in reality, Huo Shan Huang Ya is a green tea grown in the Huo Shan mountains (Anhui). When the tea is being fermented, the process blocks the enzymes responsible for oxidation and causes the young shoots to turn yellow. This in fact is where the name Huang Ya comes from (yellow shoot). Because of its sophisticated characteristics, it was offered as a tribute to the Imperial court during the Ming and Qing dynasties.

TASTING NOTES

Dry: the brilliant green leaves are narrow and elongated, and are reminiscent of a bird's tongue; the outer surface of the leaves is covered with a light down.

Liquor: golden yellow with an aroma of nuts (chestnuts, hazelnuts) and a sweet after taste.

Infusion: the leaves are light green tending to yellow, with very intense flowery notes.

PREPARATION

Western method: approx. 1/16 oz (2-3 grams) for every 2/3 cup (150 milliliters) of water at 175° F (80° C) for 2-3 minute infusion.

Eastern method: 1/8 oz (5 grams) for every 2/3 cup (150 milliliters) of water at 175° F (80° C) for 4-5 infusions of 20-30 seconds each.

Recommended with: rice, vegetables, shellfish, chicken curry, cakes and hazelnut biscuits.

LIU AN GUA PIAN

TYPE: GREEN TEA

AREA OF PROVENANCE: CHINA, ANHUI, JINZHAI

This tea was originally called Gua Zi Pian or "sunflower seed" due to its shape which resembles the popular snack served in Chinese tea houses. Over the years, the name changed to the simpler Gua Pian. Liu An refers to the village where this tea has its origins. Described by Lu Yu as a superior quality tea, it was offered as a tribute to the Imperial Court during the Ming dynasty. Only the small leaves are processed, after the shoots have been removed.

TASTING NOTES

Dry: elongated, narrow emerald green leaves.

Liquor: golden yellow; the intense sweet taste, with flowery, fruity and mildly empyreumatic notes, lingers persistently in the mouth and has great thirst-quenching properties, making it perfect on hot summer days.

Infusion: large, regularly shaped, brilliant green leaves.

PREPARATION

Western method: approx. 1/16 oz (2-3 grams) for every 2/3 cup (150 milliliters) of water at 175° F (80° C) for 2 minute infusion.

Eastern method: 1/8 oz (5 grams) for every 2/3 cup (150 milliliters) of water at 175° F (80° C) for up to 3-4 infusions of 20-30 seconds each.

Recommended with: lightly salted foods, Parma ham and melon, mixed salads and fruit salad.

GREEN TEA

JASMINE PEARL - JASMINE LONG ZHU

TYPE: SCENTED GREEN TEA

AREA OF PROVENANCE: CHINA, FUJIAN

This green, Fujian tea is hand-rolled into pearls consisting of one tender shoot and two leaves, to create a real classic with an enchanting sweet taste and a delicate jasmine aroma. The natural scent comes from contact with fresh jasmine flowers. Production of this tea takes place in two distinct phases: in spring, the leaves are processed using the same technique as for green tea; in summer, when the jasmine is in full flower, it is harvested and added to previously processed tea leaves, which then absorb the jasmine perfume. The more frequent the contact between leaf and flower, the better the quality of the tea and the higher the cost of the pearls. This sensory experience offered by this tea is an absolute must.

TASTING NOTES

Dry: small, silvery pearls with an intoxicating scent of jasmine.

Liquor: dark matt yellow; the flowery notes are intense and linger beautifully in the mouth; soft and slightly astringent to the touch.

Infusion: the rolled leaves and shoots are a brilliant light green.

PREPARATION

Western method: approx. 1/16 oz (2-3 grams) for every 2/3 cup (150 milliliters) of water at 185° F (85° C) for 2-3 minute infusion.

Eastern method: approx. 1/8 oz (5-6 grams) for every 2/3 cup (150 milliliters) of water at 185° F (85° C) for 3-5 infusions of 20-40 seconds each.

Recommended with: spicy foods, spiced white meats, shellfish, mozzarella, vegetables, potatoes, tarte tatin or carrot cake.

LONG JING

ENGLISH TRANSLITERATION: LUNG CHING
TYPE: GREEN TEA
AREA OF PROVENANCE: CHINA, ZHEJIANG, XI HU

This, the most famous of all Chinese teas, boasts over a thousand years of history, and was mentioned in the first book dedicated to tea, the famous The Classic of Tea by Lu Yu, which dates back to the Tang dynasty.

The most original and highly prized Long Jing tea is Xi Hu Long Jing, which comes from the hillsides around Xi Hu. As a food product, it is protected by Chinese law. To attain PGI status (equivalent to the Italian DOCG for wines), the whole production process, from harvesting to packaging, must take place in the area of provenance. This production area measures 168 square kilometers, meaning that this superb tea is produced in very limited quantities that barely meet the demand of the domestic market. The best harvest of Xi Hu Long Jing is known as Shi Feng and, unfortunately, is practically impossible to find outside China. It is, however, possible to sample good quality Long Jing, as its production has been gradually expanded to other provinces and it is nowadays the most grown green tea in all of China. It has an unmistakable aroma of boiled chestnuts.

TASTING NOTES

Dry: narrow, flattened olive green-yellow leaves.
Liquor: brilliant golden yellow; the taste is soft, with notes of boiled chestnut, toasted nuts and vanilla.
Infusion: the young shoots are brilliant green.

PREPARATION

Western method: approx. 1/16 oz (2-3 grams) for every 2/3 cup (150 milliliters) of water at 175° F (80° C) for 2-3 minute infusion.
Eastern method: approx. 1/8 oz (5-6 grams) for every 2/3 cup (150 milliliters) of water at 175° F (80° C) for 4-5 infusions of 20-40 seconds each.

Recommended with: vegetable soups, lightly salted foods, rice, grilled fish, shellfish, flavored cheeses (Brie and Camembert), spiced white meats and fruit.

GREEN TEA

GREEN LYCHEE

TYPE: SCENTED GREEN TEA
AREA OF PROVENANCE: CHINA, HUNAN

This green tea, scented with lychees, a native fruit of southern China and all of south-east Asia, is hand made and sold in the form of small balls. In this Hunan quality tea, the leaves are put into direct contact with fresh lychees. The flesh of this fruit is transparent and highly scented, and was always enjoyed as a delicacy by the Imperial court. The tradition of scenting teas by direct contact with fruit and flowers originated in China, though nowadays artificial aromas are added. This tea enables drinkers to experience the legacy of age-old knowledge born from patience and respect for natural products and processes.

The drink, with its enchanting, unmistakable taste and delicate but voluptuous scent, is an absolute must: it is poetry in a cup. As it can be drunk hot or cold, it is ideal in any season.

TASTING NOTES

Dry: the leaves are rolled into small balls of varying sizes, and are matt green with yellow streaks; intense scent of roses and grapes (moscato).

Liquor: clear golden yellow; the sweet hint of lychees and the flowery notes of tea leaves blend to form a unique aromatic bouquet; flower notes of rose and gardenia blend with fruity notes of apricot, dried dates and raisins.

Infusion: the dark matt green leaves open up completely, and the dominating scent is that of grapes (moscato).

PREPARATION

Western method: approx. 1/16 oz (2 grams) for every 2/3 cup (150 milliliters) of water at 185° F (85° C) for 2-3 minute infusion.

Eastern method: 3-4 balls for every 2/3 cup (150 milliliters) of water at 185° F (85° C) for 4-5 infusions of 20-40 seconds each.

Recommended with: yoghurt bavarois, Greek yoghurt and honey, vanilla desserts and custards, carrot and hazelnut cakes, white chocolate, Basmati rice, fresh fruit and fruit salad with vodka.

TAI PING HOU KUI

TYPE: GREEN TEA
AREA OF PROVENANCE: CHINA, ANHUI, HUANG SHAN

This tea is often quoted by Chinese poets from Tai Ping (Anhui), at the foot of the Huang Shan mountains. Its unique shape makes it unlike all other green teas. During processing, Tai Ping Hou Kui is neither roller nor compressed. This procedure gives it its unique, unmistakable appearance: unusually long, flattened leaves that can measure up to 6 inches (15 centimeters) in length.

HOW TO PREPARE TAI PING HOU KUI

To prepare this extraordinary tea, which is unique for more than just its refined aroma, but also because of its unusual appearance, we do not recommend a Gaiwan cup. Its leaves can grow to be even 6 inch (15 cm) long, because of which it is better to use a tall glass to prepare it or a tall glass teapot, warmed beforehand by filling them with 175-185° F (80-85° C) water. Once you have discarded the water from the cup or tall glass teapot, add approx. 1/16-1/8 oz (3-5 grams) of Tai Ping Hou Kui leaves, then pour in new water that has been brought up to temperature. If you are using the cup, you can drink the tea directly in it. If you are using a teapot, it is preferable to pour the brew into a glass jar and then serve it in cups.

TASTING NOTES

Dry: the long flat leaves are brilliant green.
Liquor: in the cup, it is a light, crystal clear color; it has a surprisingly delicate and sweet taste that is reminiscent of orchids.
Infusion: the long flat leaves lose their shine and become duller and lighter; some red veins may appear.

PREPARATION

Western method: approx. 1/16 oz (2-3 grams) for every 2/3 cup (150 milliliters) of water at 175° F (80° C) for 3 minute infusion.
Eastern method: 1/8 oz (5 grams) for every 2/3 cup (150 milliliters) of water at 175° F (80° C) for 3 infusions of 30-40 seconds each.

Recommended with: no recommendations – with its delicate orchid notes, this tea is best drunk alone.

GREEN TEA

HOW TO PREPARE BLOOMING GREEN TEAS

To enjoy the display offered by blooming green teas blossoms, we recommend choosing a tall and narrow glass cup or a tall glass teapot. The teapot or cup should be at least 6 inches (15 centimeters) tall.

After pouring water heated to around 175°-185° F (80°-85° C) on the tea "blossom," you will have to wait a few minutes before you can observe the unfurling of the truly masterful Chinese art of binding tea buds. The "tea blossoms" can be made solely of tea buds, in the case of Lu Mu Dan, or paired with different flowers, like jasmine, calendulas, amaranths, lilies, globe amaranths, or hibiscus. In addition to enriching the liquor with a delicate floral aroma, these flowers offer a striking and spectacular visual that is sure to please.
Lu Mu Dan, whose shape is similar to a chrysanthemum or small rose, can also be prepared in a glass Gaiwan cup.

GREEN TEA

GREEN TEA

The slow and delicate unfurling of "blooming teas"

GREEN TEA

LU MU DAN

TYPE: GREEN SCENTED TEA
AREA OF PROVENANCE: CHINA, ANHUI, SHE XIAN

This tea, fashioned into the shape of a flower, is made exclusively of green tea shoots from the plantations on the Huang Shan mountains in the Anhui region, and more specifically from the area of She Xian. This classic among Chinese green teas can be seen as a forerunner of the "blooming teas." These Chinese works of art were made by tying tea shoots together to create small spheres, towers and seated Buddhas.

Unlike blooming teas, in which the beauty of the budding flowers they contain is often marred by the mediocre quality of the tea leaves used, Lu Mu Dan excels. This tea is a rare example of poetry and aesthetics combining to offer truly surprising aromatic notes. After seeping for a few minutes, this delicate tea in the shape of a rose, unfurls to create a clear and brilliant sweet, honeyed liquor.

TASTING NOTES

Dry: about a hundred small shoots are tied together to form a star shaped bouquet.

Liquor: brilliant, light colored and crystal clear; the sweet, and almost never astringent taste has delicate but linger notes of honey, licorice and boiled chestnuts, typical of the best Chinese green teas.

Infusion: once allowed to steep, the shoots in the star shaped bouquet unfurl to take on a shape reminiscent of a Chrysanthemum, a carnation or a small rose.

PREPARATION

1 bouquet for every 1 1/4 cup (30 centiliters) of water at 175-185° F (80-85° C) for 2-3 minute infusion.

Recommended with: lightly salted foods, white meats, vegetables, fish, rice and fruit.

Japanese cast iron teapots keep the water hot for longer.
For this reason, they were traditionally used as kettles.

GREEN TEA - JAPAN

Tea in all its forms is so widespread in Japanese society that it forms part of almost every ritual of daily life: it is served with meals in restaurants (Bancha, Houjicha), it is prepared among friends or in small groups for refined convivial gatherings (Sencha, Gyokuro), and, of course, it epitomizes Zen philosophy during the tea ceremony (Matcha).

The annual production of green tea is not sufficient to meet domestic demand, and so a good proportion of green tea sold in Japan is not actually produced locally, but is in fact cultivated and processed in China, Vietnam or Indonesia, following traditional production methods.

In Japan, tea is harvested two to four times a year. The spring crop is undoubtedly the best and most sought after. Japanese green tea is traditionally grown in the prefecture of Shizuoka, home to the best Sencha, the prefecture of Kyoto, known for the prestigious Matcha and Gyokuro, and the prefectures of Kagoshima and Kyushu, in the south of the country.

In the past, this tea was entirely processed by hand (temomi-cha) through the expert work of Temomi Masters, who handed down their tradition from one generation to the next, as a precious treasure to be safeguarded.

Unfortunately, machinery has taken over in recent decades, but every year a national competition is held for the best temomi-cha, or handmade tea. The first thirty winners are sold at no less than 90,718 yen/lb (200,000 yen/kg).

In Japan, green tea retains its bright green color through a method of steaming developed in Kyoto in 1738 by Nagatani Soen.

During this very brief heating phase, the high temperature reached blocks the enzymes responsible for oxidation and allows the tea to maintain its original hue. This procedure also renders the leaves elastic and supple, making them easier to roll up.

Rolling takes about four hours, and is performed on a heated surface, called hoiro, until the leaves turn dark green and needle shaped.

Traditionally, the plantations devoted to the finest teas are "shaded:" during the last 20-30 days before harvesting, the plants are covered with canvas sheets to reduce exposure to the sun. This technique increases the sweetness of the tea, reducing its catechin content, and consequently limiting the astringency and bitterness typical of some green teas.

HOW TO PREPARE JAPANESE GREEN TEA

The infusion method used for Japanese green teas is a middle road between the quick and repetitive Chinese method and the prolonged, single method used in the West.

For Bancha, Houjicha, and Genmaicha teas, a single infusion is used as in the West, but it is relatively shorter.

For more valued teas such as Sencha or Gyokuro, an infusion of around 2-2.5 minutes is repeated three times.

HOW TO USE THE KYUSU TEAPOT

The Kyusu teapot is a small teapot made of various materials (porcelain, glass) with a special grid filter inside and a very ergonomic and convenient side handle.

Traditionally, it is the typical teapot used to prepare Japanese green teas. It has a very small capacity and can normally hold between 1/2 and 1 1/4 cups (100 and 300 ml) of water.

If you do not have a water boiler with temperature control, we recommend placing the Kyusu pot and three cups on the table and proceeding as follows:

1. bring the water to the boil;
2. put the tea leaves inside the teapot;
3. fill two cups with hot water, leaving the third empty;
4. use the empty cup to pour hot water from one cup to another. Each time the water is poured, its temperature lowers by around 50° F (10° C);
5. when the water has reached around 175° F (80° C) for Sencha or 140°-160° F (60°-70° C) for Gyokuro, pour the water from the two cups into to the Kyusu teapot;
6. pour the tea directly into the cups;
7. repeat the infusion up to three times, slightly reducing the time for each infusion.

BANCHA KAKEGAWA

TYPE: GREEN TEA

AREA OF PROVENANCE: JAPAN, SHIZUOKA, KAKEGAWA

Lovers of Bancha tea immediately appreciate the very high quality of this first flush Bancha, the most highly prized harvest from the plantations of Kakegawa that lie to the west of the Shizuoka prefecture. It is a must for those who don't particularly enjoy this type of tea: just one sip is enough to realize that it has nothing whatsoever to do with the common Bancha teas found on the market. It has a low tannin content and goes perfectly with meals at any time of the day.

TASTING NOTES

Dry: large intense brilliant green leaves; fruity scent with a hint of sweetness.

Liquor: yellow-green, slightly cloudy; its taste is fresh and tender with delicate herbal (spinach) and marine notes.

Infusion: the leaves are an intense dark green color; they resemble the leaves of cooked spinach.

PREPARATION

Approx. 1/16 oz (2-3 grams) for every 2/3 cup (150 milliliters) of water at 175° F (80° C) for 2 1/2 minute infusion.

Recommended with: slightly salty foods, raw and cooked fish, shellfish, vegetables and rice.

GENMAICHA

This Genmaicha comes from the Fukuroi plantations in the coastal plain to the south west of Shizuoka. It is created by blending a first flush Spring Bancha – the most prized Bancha tea – with toasted brown rice.

A legend surrounds the origins of this tea: one day back in the 15th century, a samurai was sipping a cup of tea while preparing a plan of attack with his men. His servant, Genmai, clumsily let a few grains of rice fall into the cup. Out of rage, the samurai chopped off his head. When he had calmed down, he went on sipping his tea, and realized that the tea tasted even better thanks to the scent of rice. Regretting his hasty action, from that day on the samurai only drank his tea with rice, and named this new drink Genmaicha, in honor of his dead servant. However, a far more likely story is that the population who lived far away from the plantation used to blend the tea with rice to make their stocks last longer. Whatever its origins, today Genmaicha is one of the most widespread teas in Japan.

It has an unmistakable hazelnut taste, and is also known as "popcorn teas." Its low tannin content makes it an ideal tea at any time of day, even cold.

TASTING NOTES

Dry: brilliant green leaves blended with toasted grains of rice and puffed maize (popcorn); the flower notes blend perfectly with the empyreumatic toasted ones.

Liquor: intense yellow-green; toasted rice notes blend beautifully with the sweetness from the springtime Bancha; a surprising, lingering flavor reminiscent of hazelnut.

Infusion: the leaves turn dark green and the toasted rice takes on a darker hue.

PREPARATION

Approx. 1/16 oz (2-3 grams) for every 2/3 cup (150 milliliters) of water at 175-185° F (80-85° C) for 2-2.5 minute infusion.

Recommended with: soups, rice, raw or cooked fish, shellfish, vegetables and nut biscuits.

GYOKURO

TYPE: GREEN TEA

AREA OF PROVENANCE: JAPAN, SHIZUOKA, OKABE

This is the most highly valued Japanese tea, grown near Okabe in the prefecture of Shizuoka, one of the best known areas for the cultivation of Gyokuro.

In the three weeks before the harvest, the plantation is completely covered over with special sheets to keep the plants in the shade. This technique increases the quantity of caffeine and amino acids while decreasing the catechin content of the leaves. In terms of flavor, this results in a much less astringent, bitter taste, typical of some green teas.

TASTING NOTES

Dry: dark green very thin needle-like leaves.

Liquor: green-yellow, slightly cloudy, very soft and not astringent; marine (sea food) aromas dominate, accompanied by flower notes; umami flavor.

Infusion: the leaves are an intensely brilliant dark green.

PREPARATION

Approx. 1/16 oz (2-3 grams) for every 2/3 cup (150 milliliters) of water at 140-160° F (60-70° C) for 2 1/2 minute infusion.

Recommended with: shellfish, raw and cooked fish, vegetables, fresh and soft cheeses.

HOUJICHA

TYPE: GREEN TEA
AREA OF PROVENANCE: JAPAN, SHIZUOKA, FUKUROI

This very special Japanese tea is a Bancha that has been delicately toasted.

The best Houjicha is made with leaves harvested in the autumn from the Fukuroi plantations in the coastal plain to the south-west of Shizuoka.
It is a very delicate tea, containing almost no tannin, making it ideal at any time of day and suitable for children. Houjicha goes perfectly with any type of dish.

TASTING NOTES

Dry: long, large, intense hazelnut and amber colored leaves, which give off a sophisticated toasted and flowery aroma, with woody and slightly fruity notes.
Liquor: a brilliant warm brown with shades of old gold; the tea release an aromatic taste in the mouth which is reminiscent of toasted hazelnuts, providing a lingering malty after taste.
Infusion: dark, nearly black khaki color with a scent dominated by fruit, woody notes, with a hint of spiciness.

PREPARATION

Approx. 1/16 oz (2-3 grams) for every 2/3 cup (150 milliliters) of water at 175-185° F (80 -85° C) for 2-3 minute infusion.

Recommended with: grilled fish, mollusks, pork, vegetables, rice, hazelnut pies and biscuits.

GREEN TEA

KUKICHA

TYPE: GREEN TEA

AREA OF PROVENANCE: JAPAN, SHIZOUKA, KAKEGAWA

Kukicha is generally a tea whose main ingredients come from the least valued part of the plant, the stems.

In this particular case, the Kukicha is the unusual result of processing with a Sencha first flush from the plantations at Kakegawa (Shizuoka). The outcome is surprising for its unique taste and freshness, and for the unexpected harmony it offers the senses. It is the perfect starting point for a journey of discovery about Japanese green teas, as it helps us to overcome any prejudices we may have about their herbal flavor being an acquired taste.

TASTING NOTES

Dry: a lovely, light green assortment of stems, which release a fresh, clean scent with harmoniously delicate flowery notes.

Liquor: natural brilliant green in color, and delicate, with a smooth velvety surface; in the cup, is refreshing, aromatic flavor and seductive notes will delight tea aficionados.

Infusion: the stems take on a brilliant green hue with hints of yellow.

PREPARATION

Approx. 1/16 oz (2-3 grams) for every 2/3 cup (150 milliliters) of water at 175° F (80° C) for 2-3 minute infusion.

Recommended with: rice, vegetables, cheeses (Asiago, Fontainebleau), fish cooked with ginger and lemon grass, and as an accompaniment to Sunday brunch.

SENCHA KAGOSHIMA

TYPE: GREEN TEA

AREA OF PROVENANCE: JAPAN, KAGOSHIMA, KOYU

Sencha is Japan's most famous tea and represents nearly 80% of national tea production with varying levels of quality. This tea has a characteristic fresh scent thanks to a special processing procedure that involves a three-fold steam cooking process.

The best Senchas are rich in amino acids and vitamin C. The first harvest in April is considered the best and is called Shincha, or "new tea."

This superb Sencha tea comes from the Kagoshima prefecture at the southernmost tip of Japan. The flavor is fresh and less astringent than the usual Senchas and is very similar to Gyokuro. Its refreshing qualities make it ideal for drinking in the early summer.

TASTING NOTES

Dry: long regularly shaped needle-like jade green leaves; fresh green grass scent with an aquatic top note.

Liquor: dark green, soft on the palate, only slightly astringent with a mild sweet taste and refreshing flowery scents; the first warm rays of the spring sun reflect in its flavor.

Infusion: very tender leaves, similar to cooked spinach, with grassy, cooked vegetable notes.

PREPARATION

Approx. 1/16 oz (2-3 grams) for every 2/3 cup (150 milliliters) of water at 175° F (80° C) for 2 1/2 minute infusion.

Recommended with: raw and cooked fish, mollusks and shellfish, rice, both raw and cooked vegetables, fresh delicate cheeses, light pulse soups, traditional Japanese azuki bean-based desserts.

CHA NO YU:
THE ANCIENT JAPANESE ART OF TEA MAKING

The Japanese tea ritual is closely connected with the spread of Buddhism. In the twelfth century, a monk named Eisai, on returning from a trip to China, brought home the seeds of the tea plant, and introduced the Chinese method of preparing tea in use during the Song dynasty. At that time, the tea leaves were compressed and then stone milled to make a fine powder. The drink, therefore, was prepared by dissolution rather than infusion. This technique, now outmoded in China, is still used in Japan today.

Tea was a great hit at the imperial court, and outside the court, its preparation became widespread in monasteries. By taking this energy drink, monks could stay awake during their long hours of meditation.

Soon, precise tea making rules – and even competitions – began to take hold. All this greatly attracted the feudal lords and warriors who dominated medieval society at the time. These early rituals may be considered the precursors of the Cha No Yu, or Japanese tea ceremony.

At his home in Kyoto, Murata Shuko created a tea room from four and a half tatami, where he developed the first Cha No Yu rules. However, it was only with the Master Sen no Rikyu (1522-1591) that the art of tea making became a veritable ritual with encoded gestures.

The Cha No Yu tea ceremony revolved around Matcha, a finely ground green tea used to this day.

Cha No Yu, Japanese for "hot tea water," is a ceremony blending harmony, respect, purity and tranquility. The ceremony takes place in the tea room, or "place of emptiness," reached after crossing a garden path paved with flat and irregular stones. The master (or mistress), kneeling on the tatami mat like his guests, dries the tea bowl (chawan) with a silk cloth hanging from his kimono belt. With a bamboo spatula (chashaku), he pours a small amount of powdered green Matcha tea into the bowl. With a bamboo ladle (hishaku), he takes hot water from an iron kettle and pours it into the bowl, on top of the tea. To obtain the so-called "jade froth," he stirs the tea vigorously with a special bamboo whisk (chasen).

The Matcha is now ready to be served to the first guest. The same ceremony is repeated for each guest, serving each cup with a small traditional dessert.

It takes years, even decades, of study to learn the art of the Japanese tea ceremony. The masters believe that, to succeed, it is important to understand the true spirit of tea.

MATCHA

TYPE: GREEN TEA

AREA OF PROVENANCE: JAPAN, AICHI, NISHIO

Matcha is a traditional Japanese green tea used in the Cha No Yu tea ceremony.

Some of the best green Matcha teas come from the practically uncontaminated area of Nishio, in the Aichi prefecture, where tea has been produced since the 1200s. These teas are obtained from much greener and more nutrient-rich leaves than those found in other areas of the country.

Matcha is the only tea prepared from powdered leaves, which, instead of being infused, are dissolved in hot water. This tea has better anti-oxidizing and energy giving properties than other green teas. Less highly prized Matcha teas are used widely in gourmet cooking, especially in baking.

TASTING NOTES

Dry: powder fine, it is a shiny emerald green with a scent of the uncontaminated forest.

Liquor: intensely green and cloudy, the famous "jade froth" on the surface offers a very special tactile sensation as you sip it; its sour taste is reminiscent of the sweet notes of flours and leaves a lingering, slightly bitter after taste in the mouth, with subtle scent of herbs and newly mown hay.

PREPARATION

Put about 1/16 oz (1 gram) of tea (i.e. the tip of a teaspoon or the amount held in a chashaku, or bamboo spatula) into the dish. Pour in hot water at about 160°-175° F (70°-80° C) then stir vigorously with a "chasen" until a dense foam appears.

Recommended with: caviar, oysters, white chocolate, delicate pastries, egg and mascarpone based creams, and to prepare smoothies and soy milk milkshakes, or sprinkle over soft cheeses.

YELLOW TEA

Yellow tea is a Chinese specialty produced in limited quantities. It owes its name to the typical color of its leaves and liquor. It is perhaps the type of tea least known to the general public, partly because its limited production makes real yellow tea very expensive and difficult to find outside the motherland.

This specialty is mainly produced in the Hunan region of China, and in particular on the island of Jun Shan, home to the original yellow tea.

From the point of view of production, it is very similar to green tea, from which it originated quite by accident.

The main characteristic that distinguishes yellow tea from green tea is the – now intentional – yellowing of its leaves during processing, due to light oxidation.

The basic techniques for processing yellow tea are: heating, rolling, covering and drying.

During the first phase, the leaves are softened in a cauldron on high heat to reduce their level of hydration.

Then, the leaves are rolled to release their essential oils and give them their shape.

So far, the processing technique is identical to that used for green tea. The next step is crucial, determining the quality of the finished product and enabling the tea to be classified as lightly oxidized yellow tea.

The leaves are stacked in large piles and covered: this gives them their typical yellow color.

The final drying phase, common to all types of tea, turns the leaves even more yellow.

Many tea varieties are sold in China under this name, although not strictly speaking yellow teas. This may be explained by making a small foray into the history and tradition of tea: yellow was the color symbolizing imperial power, and hence this adjective was often given to the best crops of green or white tea, sent as a tribute to the imperial court. "Imperial" teas, therefore, were referred to as yellow teas.

For the optimal storage of grand cru tea leaves, we recommend using airtight containers that protect them from light, moisture and odors.

HOW TO PREPARE YELLOW TEA

To prepare yellow tea, we recommend using glass, specifically a Gaiwan teacup or a tall and narrow glass.

For either case, it is important that the water temperature is between 175°-185° F (80°-85° C).

If you are using a Gaiwan teacup, it should be heated beforehand and then filled by one-third with tea leaves. According to your personal taste, you can do one 3-4 minute infusion, or up to 4 brief infusions, around 30-40 seconds each.

If you are using a tall and narrow glass, after it has been heated, fill it around one-third of the way full. Next, add the tea leaves and then the remaining 70% of hot water. The tea buds will slowly travel to the bottom of the glass, staying vertical. They will begin to move slightly, almost dancing, which this method of preparation allows to be enjoyed particularly well.

YELLOW TEA

JUN SHAN YIN ZHEN

TYPE: YELLOW TEA

AREA OF PROVENANCE: CHINA, HUNAN, ISLAND OF JUN SHAN

Jun Shan Yin Zhen yellow tea takes its name from the island by the same name that lies in the Hunan region of China. Thanks to the beauty of its surroundings, the island is also nick-named "the island of love." This enchanting location is where yellow tea was originally produced. Production is very limited and the tea fetches very high prices. Just to give some idea of how selective harvesting is, it takes at least five kilos of leaves to produce one kilo of dry tea.

TASTING NOTES

Dry: the tender leaves are the shape of needles and have a regular appearance, with yellow and silver tips.

Liquor: pale yellow with a fresh and lingering aroma that is reminiscent of flowers and nuts; very soft and velvety to the touch.

Infusion: the steeped tea, consisting of one shoot and one leaf, is brilliant green and keeps its nutty notes (chestnut and hazelnut).

PREPARATION

Western method: approx. 1/16 oz (2-3 grams) for every 2/3 cup (150 milliliters) of water at 175-185° F (80-85° C) for 3 minute infusion.

Eastern method: 1/8 oz (5 grams) for every 2/3 cup (150 milliliters) of water at 175-185° F (80-85° C) for 3-4 infusions of 30-40 seconds each.

Recommended with: an excellent tea to accompany meals and combines beautifully with fresh cheeses and white meats.

MENG DING HUANG YA (YELLOW YA)

TYPE: YELLOW TEA
AREA OF PROVENANCE: CHINA, SICHUAN

This very rare yellow tea has an ancient history. It was first produced in the Han dynasty more than two thousand years ago and was elected the Imperial tea during the Tang dynasty.

It is grown at the peak of the Meng mountain in Sichuan, where fog frequently enshrouds the tea gardens. Only the leaves harvested from the mist-laden slopes of this mountain can be used to produce the original Meng Ding Huang Ya. Given the small size of the production area, only very limited quantities are available, and it is rare to find this tea outside China. If you do, you'll be delighted by the unique experience it offers.

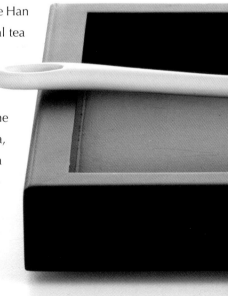

YELLOW TEA

Dry: the tender yellowy leaves have a delicate appearance and are regularly shaped.

Liquor: during infusion, the shoots remain suspended vertically in the water, creating the illusion of an elegant dance; pale yellow color with a sweet taste and notes of hazelnuts and herbs.

Infusion: the open leaves reveal a layout typical of the most highly prized harvests: one shoot and one leaf; the nutty notes (hazelnut and chestnut) linger persistently on the palate.

PREPARATION

Western method: approx. 1/16 oz (2-3 grams) for every 2/3 cup (150 milliliters) of water at 175-185° F (80 -85° C) for 3 minute infusion.

Eastern method: 1/8 oz (5 grams) for every 2/3 cup (150 milliliters) of water at 175-185° F (80-85° C) for 3-4 infusions of 30-40 seconds each.

Recommended with: thanks to its exceptional flavor, it is best drunk alone; however, it can be drunk as an accompaniment to light dishes based on white meats, nuts and baked pastries.

*Ruyao style tea set, appreciated since the times of the Song dynasty
for the characteristic cracks in the surface enamel, considered of great value.*

WHITE TEA

In the past, white tea was offered as a tribute to high dignitaries and members of the Chinese court, in witness of its uniqueness and value.

Top-rate white tea depends on the botanical specimen used, the processing method adopted, and the presence of abundant white down on the buds.

As downy shoots and leaves are used for this kind of tea, the pale yellow liquor tastes velvety smooth in the mouth, marked by a full, fresh aroma.

A simple yet very special method is used to process white tea.

Its preparation does not involve heating or rolling, the only techniques used being withering and drying.

The most precious variety is composed exclusively of shoots that, once harvested, are arranged on shelves in special ventilated rooms (or exposed to the sun when the temperature is mild), where they are left until they reach the desired level of withering.

After this phase, which may last a few days, the leaves are dried in large baskets at low temperatures, until completely dehydrated.

Native to the Fujian region of China, top-rate white tea is also produced in limited quantities outside the homeland, for example in Ruhuna, in south Sri Lanka.

HOW TO PREPARE WHITE TEA

For the optimal preparation of white tea, we recommend a glass or porcelain Gai-wan cup.

It is good to use water that is from 165°-175° F (75°-80° C), carefully warming the cup beforehand, emptying it, and then filling it one-third of the way with water that has been heated to the temperature to be used for the first infusion. At this point, add the tea leaves and fill the cup completely with more hot water.

If you prefer a brew with a more distinct and intense taste, opt for a single infusion of around 5-10 minutes, or perform up to 3 brief infusions around 30-60 seconds each if you enjoy a more fresh, light, and delicate taste.

These preparation times are longer with respect to other types of tea because white tea is not processed by rolling. During the infusion, the aromas and essential oils within the tea leaves are not immediately released, as they require longer times to be released.

In order to understand all of the subtle and delicate shades of the aromas of this family of tea, the Eastern method of infusion with repeated infusions is definitely preferable over the single European infusion.

BAI HAO YIN ZHEN

TYPE: WHITE TEA
AREA OF PROVENANCE: CHINA, FUJIAN, FUDING

Bai Hao Yin Zhen, also known as "silver needle," is a white tea produced in China in the province of Fujian. Among the most highly prized white teas, it is made exclusively with shoots that have not yet opened. This is where white tea reaches perfection.

The best harvests, which are all performed by hand, come from the mountainous plantations of Tai Lao, in the region of Fuding (where the white tea Yin Zhen was originally produced). This area enjoys a mild sub-tropical climate with high humidity all year round and abundant rain. The perfect climatic conditions favor the growth of this wonder of nature, which provides a crystal clear, velvety infusion with notes of honey and a light flowery flavor. Bai Hao Yin Zhen has always been considered a unique tea. By tradition, part of the harvest was set aside as a tribute to the Emperor, and still today it is one of the most highly prized and expensive teas in existence. The care with which unopened shoots are chosen and the delicacy of its aroma make it a tea for real aficionados. Only a refined, expert palate can fully appreciate the subtle taste of this tea. It is a tea for meditation, best savored on its own without the distraction of food.

TASTING NOTES
Dry: large unopened shoots covered with silvery down; as soft to the touch as edelweiss petals.
Liquor: pale yellow; soft, velvety and a perfect balance of very delicate aromas which blend in total harmony.
Infusion: the young shoots are light green.

PREPARATION
Western method: approx. 1/16 oz (2-3 grams) for every 2/3 cup (150 milliliters) of water at 165-175° F (75-80° C) for 5-10 minute infusion.
Eastern method: 1/8 oz (5 grams) for every (150 milliliters) of water at 165-175° F (75-80° C) for up to 3 infusions of 30-60 seconds each.

Recommended with: nothing. Its delicate taste is best appreciated on its own.

WHITE TEA

BAI MU DAN

TYPE: WHITE TEA

AREA OF PROVENANCE: CHINA, FUJIAN, ZHENG HE

Bai Mu Dan, also known as White Peony, is a white tea made with one shoot and two open leaves. Bai Mu Dan is sometimes preferred by white tea drinkers for its full and intense flavor, in comparison with other much more delicate white teas.

It comes from the plantations in Zheng He in the province of Fujian, where Bai Mu Dan was originally cultivated. This tea stands out for the soft, honeyed delicacy of its aroma. The intensity of its velvety note and lingering flavor make it the ideal choice for all those who wish to discover this family of teas.

TASTING NOTES

Dry: large unopened shoots covered with dense silvery down and open down-covered leaves.
Liquor: pale yellow; its delicate flowery, fresh and velvety notes are suggestive of honey; compared with Bai Hao Yin Zhen, its taste is stronger, more intense and lingering.
Infusion: the leaves and shoots are light green.

PREPARATION

Western method: approx. 1/16 oz (2-3 grams) for every 2/3 cup (150 milliliters) of water at 165-175° F (75-80° C) for 5-10 minute infusion.
Eastern method: 1/8 oz (5 grams) for every 2/3 cup (150 milliliters) of water at 165-175° F (75-80° C) for up to 3 infusions of 30-60 seconds each.

Recommended with: ideal on its own as a tea for meditation or combined with light vegetable based meals, white meats, fish or fresh soft cheeses or semi-soft cheeses like Asiago.

RUHUNA SILVER TIPS

TYPE: WHITE TEA

AREA OF PROVENANCE: SRI LANKA, RUHUNA, MATARA DISTRICT

One of Sri Lanka's best teas and a source of great national pride. For a long time this tea was only intended for kings and tea experts. The leaves are harvested and processed by hand, and only shoots which have not yet opened are taken.

The best buds are harvested in March, April and at the beginning of May. The leaves are only lightly oxidized thanks a process of drying in the sun, with no use made of mechanical drying systems. Although Silver Tips is a white tea, it has a special character with delicate balsamic, spicy base notes which, according to some, are reminiscent of the classic white teas of Sri Lanka.

TASTING NOTES

Dry: the large shoots are very soft, enshrouded in a velvety silvery-white down, and with an intense scent of honey.

Liquor: intense yellow tending to golden brown in prolonged infusions; stands out for its fresh and delicate scent, has a distinct flavor with pronounced notes of honey and a hint of pine – pure silk on the palate.

Infusion: large blemish-free shoots tending to white, with honeyed and empyreumatic notes.

PREPARATION

Western method: approx. 1/8 oz (3-5 grams) for every 2/3 cup (150 milliliters) of water at 175° F (80° C) for 5-7 minute infusion.

Recommended with: best drunk alone for its sublime taste or as an accompaniment to light white meat based dishes, blue-veined cheeses or fish.

WHITE TEA

BLUE-GREEN OR WULONG
TEA - CHINA

*Yi Xing terracotta teapot. With use, its porous surface absorbs the aromas of the teas
and, in time, enhances the fragrance of quality teas.*

This family of teas, better known as Wulong teas (also spelt Oolong, which in Chinese means "black dragon"), comprises a series of teas whose leaves undergo partial oxidation during processing. Different types of product may be obtained, each with unique organoleptic characteristics, depending on the desired intensity.

Low levels of oxidation produce Wulongs similar to green tea, with distinct floral notes.

High levels of oxidation, on the other hand, produce decidedly darker and fruitier Wulongs, very similar to red tea. These teas originate in the Chinese province of Fujian, where they were first produced around 400 years ago. To this day, the most traditional Wulongs come from this region, as well as Guangdong and Taiwan.

The Wulong of Fujan is produced both in the north and south of the province, and is represented by the Wuyi Yan Cha and Anxi Tie Guan Yin varieties. The Fenghuang Dancong botanical specimen is typical of Gaungdong, while the Taiwan Wulongs are obtained by processing the Bao Zhong specimen.

The production of Wulong teas is a complex matter: leaves are left to wither in the sun, then air dried, rotated, heated, rolled and finally dried once more. The production process is basically a combination of the processes used for the production of green and oxidized teas.

Freshly picked leaves are scattered on canvases and exposed to sunlight to allow part of their moisture to evaporate. This drying process is also called sun withering. Next, air drying phases – during which the leaves are spread in workshops over bamboo baskets, to release the heat – are alternated with phases of rotation, performed either manually or with the aid of machinery. This process causes friction between the leaves, darkening their edges. Once the desired level of oxidation has been reached, the leaves are heated to block the enzyme activity responsible for oxidation.

Next, various rolling methods may be applied, depending on the type of Wulong required. Rotary movements release essential oils from the leaves and help to give them their typical rolled or twisted shape. At this point, the leaves are ready for the final drying phase, initially conducted at a high temperature for a short period of time, and then at a low temperature for a decidedly longer time.

There are many legends concerning the origins of Wulong tea and its name, which in Chinese means black dragon. However, they all relate of the accidental discovery of partial oxidation caused by the momentary abandonment, for one reason or another, of the harvested tea leaves.

HOW TO PREPARE WULONG TEA

The best accessories to prepare Wulong tea are a porcelain Gaiwan teacup and a terracotta Yi Xing teapot. The downside of a porcelain Gaiwan teacup is that it is a good conductor of heat. High-temperature water, around 195-205° F (90-95° C), will quickly overheat the cup's lid, with the risk of burning your fingers. If you are not acquainted with using a Gaiwan teacup, it is better to opt for a terracotta Yi Xing teapot.

The method of preparation practiced in China and Taiwan is the Gong Fu Cha technique.
Even today, this ritual is scarcely known in the West, and it is definitely the best way to appreciate the aromas as it allows for the tea leaves to release and express their entire potential for each infusion.

SHORT LESSON IN GONG FU CHA

1. Heat the water to 195-205° F (90-95° C). For Wulong teas that have a low oxidation or for teas whose leaves are not curled, the water must have a slightly lower temperature of around 185-195° F (85-90° C).

2. Place the equipment on the ceremonial table along with the tray to catch liquids. This includes the terracotta teapot, jar, and teacups (the set is composed of a tall cup to experience the scent and a short cup to taste the tea).

3. Pour the water into the teapot to heat it.

4. Pour the water into the jar to heat it.

5. Put the tea leaves into the teapot (around 1/4 or 1/3 the volume of the teapot) using the wooden tea measuring spoon. To more easily add the leaves into the teapot, it might be useful to use the wooden funnel.

6. Pour water into the teapot and briefly rinse the leaves for around 10 seconds. Then empty the teapot and discard the rinse water. This step only serves to wet and soften the leaves to better prepare them for future infusions that you will drink.

7. Once the teapot is filled, close it with the lid. Wait around 30-40 seconds, continuing to pour hot water onto the teapot to prevent it from cooling.

8. Pour the brew from the pot into the jar. During this step, it might be useful to use the strainer to avoid that leaves or parts of leaves are poured into the cups.

9. Pour the brew into the tall aromatizing cups, and then into the short tasting cups. Smell the cup for its aroma, as even if it is empty it will release all of the tea's fragrance. Then taste the tea, drinking the entire contents of the short cup in three small sips.

Wulong teas yield up to 5-7 infusions. Each infusion will be different from the others, creating a more delicate or more intense brew. We recommend that you take the time to experiment, as the goal of the Gong Fu Cha method is to prepare tea in the best way possible.

DA HONG PAO

TYPE: WULONG TEA

AREA OF PROVENANCE: CHINA, FUJIAN, WUYI SHAN

Da Hong Pao is the most famous of the Wulong teas produced in the mountainous area of WuYi Shan, to the north of Fujian.

This UNESCO protected, uncontaminated area also produces Yan Cha rock teas, among which Da Hong Pao is without doubt the best, to the point that it is known as "the king of WuYi Shan." This classic tea is produced from clones obtained from cuttings of four surviving parent plants dating back to the Ming dynasty. A few kilos of tea leaves are harvested and processed from these four plants each year. This minuscule quantity is sold at a truly astronomical price, with each kilo going for tens of thousands of dollars. This is a real luxury item for a fortunate few! This mountain tea has a full body and intoxicating aroma, and can take up to 8-10 infusions. It is quite simply a must for lovers of Wulong teas.

TASTING NOTES

Dry: dark brown large leaves which are lightly rolled along their length.

Liquor: dark orange; in the mouth, the taste is rounded, with a complex bouquet of perfectly balanced notes of fruit, spices, flowers, leather, sandalwood and tobacco.

Infusion: the very dark leaves have shades of brown and black.

PREPARATION

Western method: approx. 1/16 oz (2-3 grams) for every 2/3 cup (150 milliliters) of water at 195-205° F (90-95° C) for 5 minute infusion.

Eastern method: 1/8 oz (5 grams) for every 2/3 cup (150 milliliters) of water at 195-205° F (90-95° C) for up to 8-10 infusions of 30-50 seconds each, preceded by a quick rinse of the leaves.

Recommended with: red meats, spicy foods, salty foods (e.g. cold cuts), smoked fish, pasta with meat or vegetable fillings.

FENG HUANG DAN CONG

TYPE: WULONG TEA

AREA OF PROVENANCE: CHINA, GUANGDONG, CHAOZHOU

Unlike most Wulong teas, Feng Huang Dan Cong is not produced in Fujian, but comes from the bordering region of Guangdong. As is often the case in China, the origins of the most prized and expensive teas are shrouded in mystery. The tea's name in Chinese means "tree of the Feng Huang mountains."

It is harvested directly from gigantic ancient tea plants that grow wild in a forest containing at least 3,000 plants, all of which are more than a hundred years old. The oldest plants only have one or two branches that still produce leaves. For this reason, harvests of this low oxidation Wulong only produce very limited quantities of tea, each of which has its own unique characteristics. It was only in the early 60s that a new method of cultivation was developed that gave characteristics very similar to those of the centuries old plants, but with much improved productivity.

TASTING NOTES

Dry: the light green-beige leaves are lightly rolled along their length.

Liquor: golden yellow; on the palate, the flavor is dense, velvety and almost oily, with intense flowery notes and suggestions of exotic fruit and ripe, spiced peaches.

Infusion: the large leaves are matt green with hints of red along the edges.

PREPARATION

Western method: approx. 1/16 oz (2-3 grams) for every 2/3 cup (150 milliliters) of water at 185-195° F (85-90° C) for 5 minute infusion.

Eastern method: 1/8 oz (5 grams) for every 2/3 cup (150 milliliters) of water at 185-195° F (85-90° C) for up to 5-6 infusions of 30-40 seconds each, preceded by a quick rinse of the leaves.

Recommended with: lightly salted foods, spicy foods, shellfish, fish or vegetables tempura, pork, fresh cheeses, fruit, apple pie, milk or white chocolate.

BLUE-GREEN OR WULONG TEA

HUANG JIN GUI

TYPE: WULONG TEA

AREA OF PROVENANCE: CHINA, FUJIAN, ANXI

Huang Jin Gui Wulong tea from Anxi (Fujian) is a less famous "cousin" of Tie Guan Yin, known the world over. It is made from a botanical variety known as Huang Dan and undergoes mild oxidization through the same processes as Tie Guan Yin, which gives it its flowery notes.

In China, it is considered a historical tea, its origins dating back to the Qing dynasty. Over the last few decades, the success of Tie Guan Yin, which is produced in the same area, has overshadowed this Wulong tea of undisputed quality. It was only recently rediscovered, and now enjoys the attention and appreciation it truly merits. It is an excellent tea for the afternoon or for accompanying meals.

TASTING NOTES

Dry: light green leaves tightly rolled into small pearl shapes.
Liquor: pale golden yellow; an explosion of flowery notes (osmanthus), butter and vanilla; velvet to the palate.
Infusion: the brilliant green rolled leaves are large and regularly shaped.

PREPARATION

Western method: approx. 1/16 oz (2-3 grams) for every 2/3 cup (150 milliliters) of water at 185-195° F (85-90° C) for 5 minute infusion.
Eastern method: 1/8 oz (5 grams) for every 2/3 cup (150 milliliters) of water at 185-195° F (85-90° C) for up to 5-6 infusions of 20-40 seconds each, preceded by a quick rinse of the leaves.

Recommended with: lightly salted foods, shellfish, cheeses (brie and camembert), fruit (strawberries)..

SHUI XIAN - WATER SPRITE

TYPE: WULONG TEA

AREA OF PROVENANCE: CHINA, FUJIAN, WUYI SHAN

Shui Xian and Tie Guan Yin are very popular varieties of Wulong teas in China, and are among the favorites for the Gong Fu Cha tea ceremony. Shui Xian can be found on the menus of most Chinese restaurants, and is usually indicated with the "Shui Hsien" character. It comes from the high mountains of WuYi Shan, synonymous with high quality Wulong tea.

Wulong teas from the WuYi mountains are also known as "Yan Cha," or "Tea rock," due to the rocky terrain in and around the tea gardens.

Rich in mineral salts, this is a strong Wulong with a full-bodied flavor and a fresh, fruity, flowery after taste. When the quality is mediocre, the toasted, woody notes dominate. Its leaves are larger than those of other Wulong teas.

TASTING NOTES

Dry: very long leaves which, by tradition, are rolled and, due to the high degree of oxidation, are dark anthracite in color.

Liquor: bronze; in quality Shui Xian teas, the smoked, woody, fruity and orchid notes are beautifully balanced and linger on the palate.

Infusion: very large leathery leaves.

PREPARATION

Western method: approx. 1/16 oz (2-3 grams) for every 2/3 cup (150 milliliters) of water at 190-205° F (90-95° C) for 5 minute infusion.

Eastern method: 1/8 oz (5 grams) for every 2/3 cup (150 milliliters) of water at 190-205° F (90-95° C) for up to 5-6 infusions of 30-60 seconds each, preceded by a quick rinse of the leaves.

Recommended with: red meats, soft pressed cheeses such as Gruyere or Emmental, pasta with meat or vegetarian filling.

TIE GUAN YIN

TYPE: WULONG TEA

AREA OF PROVENANCE: CHINA, FUJIAN, ANXI

Tie Guan Yin is used in the Gong Fu Cha tea ceremony, and is without any doubt the most famous Chinese Wulong tea. It comes from Anxi in the Fujian region, where it has been grown for thousands of years.

The fact that it is only 10-15% oxidized gives it very fresh, flowery notes. It is not astringent, and its excellent thirst quenching qualities and low tannin content make it ideal for drinking at any time of day. Its intense scent and lack of lingering after taste cleanse the mouth and enhance the flavor of food. Tie Guan Yin is perfect for drinking between one course and the next. The success of this tea over the last few decades has made it one of the most widely produced teas in China. Quality, however, can often suffer, and it is frequently grown far from its area of origin.

TASTING NOTES

Dry: brilliant green leaves which are tightly rolled to form pearls.
Liquor: golden, oily and extremely soft and velvety, characterized by a rich, lingering and intoxicating flowery bouquet (jasmine, magnolia, orchid, lily of the valley, wisteria, wild flowers).
Infusion: very large dark green leaves.

PREPARATION

Western method: approx. 1/16 oz (2-3 grams) for every 2/3 cup (150 milliliters) of water at 185-195° F (85-90° C) for 4 minute infusion.
Eastern method: approx. 1/8 oz (5-6 grams) for every 2/3 cup (150 milliliters) of water at 185-195° F (85-90° C) for up to 5-7 infusions of 30-40 seconds each preceded by a quick rinse of the leaves.

Recommended with: spicy foods, lightly salted dishes based on vegetables, rice or white meats. Also excellent with a snack of oven-baked delicacies.

*The glass jug and small tasting cup are essential accessories when preparing
Wulong tea following the Gong Fu Cha method*

BLUE-GREEN OR WULONG TEA - TAIWAN

Taiwan produces some of the best Wulong teas in the world.

The first tea plants, which originated in the Chinese province of Fujian, were planted in north Taiwan towards the end of the 1700s. Here, a mild and humid climate (with temperatures below 82° F (28° C) in summer and above 55° F (13° C) in winter) and heavy rainfalls offer the optimal conditions for the production of high quality Wulong tea.

From the onset, tea in this area was cultivated for exportation, especially to the United States and Japan, and, indeed, during the early 80s, about 80% of the tea produced in Taiwan was exported. In recent years, producers have become increasingly aware of the quality of their tea, and have begun to direct sales towards the local rather than the foreign market. Enormous efforts have been made to obtain products of extraordinary quality, such as Grand Cru and organic teas.

The semi-oxidized Wulong teas of Taiwan can be split into three categories: low-oxidation teas (e.g. Bao Zhong), pearl-shaped rolled teas (e.g. Ding Dong, Jin Xuan, and scented Osmanthus and Bergamot teas), and high-oxidation teas (e.g. Bai Hao Wulong). The main areas of production are the Nantou and Taipei counties, the villages of Beipu and Emei in the north-west of the island, and finally the Ali Shan mountains.

BAO ZHONG

TYPE: WULONG TEA

AREA OF PROVENANCE: TAIWAN, NANTOU, AOWANDA

This blue-green tea from the county of Nantou grows in mountain gardens at an altitude of about 4,595 feet (1,400 meters). Bao Zhong is a specialty of the north and central part of the island. Thanks to its delicious taste, it has become a much loved Wulong, not just in Taiwan but also in China and Europe. Production of this tea is currently being increased.

The dark green leaves have been 20% oxidized and produce a light, fresh liquor that is similar to green tea. The aroma is unmistakable but subtle, and followed by a sweet after taste. Its low tannin content makes it an ideal tea for any time of day.

TASTING NOTES

Dry: very large, dark green open leaves, lightly rolled along their length.
Liquor: pale golden yellow; in the mouth, the tea is very sweet, fresh and flowery (jasmine and rose).
Infusion: the leaves are dark green tending to brown at the edges.

PREPARATION

Western method: approx. 1/16 oz (2-3 grams) for every 2/3 cup (150 milliliters) of water at 185-195° F (85-90° C) for 5 minute infusion.
Eastern method: 1/8 oz (5 grams) for every 2/3 cup (150 milliliters) of water at 185-195° F (85-90° C) for up to 4-5 infusions of 20-30 seconds each preceded by a quick rinse of the leaves.

Recommended with: lightly salted foods, spicy food, fish, poultry, eggs, pork, vegetables, sweets with honey, sweet and salty crêpes, fruit salad (also excellent served cold with fruit).

BLUE-GREEN OR WULONG TEA

DONG DING

TYPE: WULONG TEA

AREA OF PROVENANCE: TAIWAN, NANTOU, AOWANDA

This classic, one of the best Wulongs from Taiwan, is named after the Dong Ding mountain in the Nantou region. The tea gardens sit at an altitude of 1400 meters in an unbelievably beautiful natural setting that is famous for its maple forests, which every autumn explode with color. In Chinese "Dong ding" means "icy peak," the name of the mountain where the cultivation of tea plants from the WuYi Shan mountain range (Fujian, China) has been in widespread practice since the late 19th century.

The Dong Ding Wulong is 30% oxidized, and the tea it produces is sweet, fresh and particularly aromatic. With its low tannin content, it is an ideal afternoon or evening tea.

TASTING NOTES

Dry: the leaves are tightly rolled and intense dark green in color.
Liquor: dark yellow in the cup, its particular aroma features top leather and tobacco notes that slowly evolve into very intense flowery-vanilla middle notes.
Infusion: the open leaf is surprisingly big.

PREPARATION

Western method: approx. 1/16 oz (2-3 grams) for every 2/3 cup (150 milliliters) of water at 195-205° F (90-95° C) for 5 minute infusion
Eastern method: 1/8 oz (5 grams) for every 2/3 cup (150 milliliters) of water at 195-205° F (90-95° C) for up to 5-7 infusions of 30-40 seconds each preceded by a quick rinse of the leaves.

Recommended with: this is a very versatile tea The sweet notes of vanilla go perfectly with lemon biscuits, crème caramel and chocolate. Its softness makes it ideal with spicy foods, blue-veined cheeses, salmon, carpaccio and lamb.

HIGH MOUNTAIN JIN XUAN (MILKY WULONG)

TYPE: WULONG TEA

AREA OF PROVENANCE: TAIWAN, NANTOU, AOWANDA

The garden in which this tea is grown is situated in the Nantou region and sits at an altitude of 4,595 feet (1,400 meters). The tea is 20% oxidized and is produced from a new variety of plant created for the cultivation of Dong Ding. However, the difference between this equally famous Wulong tea and the High Mountain Jin Xuan lies in the latter's more buttery milky notes, earning it the name of Milky Wulong.

TASTING NOTES

Dry: yellow-green leaves, tightly rolled to form pearls.

Liquor: golden yellow, crystal clear; soft and velvety, with no astringent after taste and with very intense "confiserie" notes (caramel, butter, condensed milk); delicate, lingering flavor.

Infusion: large, light green leaves; flowery notes prevail.

PREPARATION

Western method: approx. 1/16 oz (2-3 grams) for every 2/3 cup (150 milliliters) of water at 195° F (90° C) for 5 minute infusion.

Eastern method: approx. 1/8 oz (5-6 grams) for every 2/3 cup (150 milliliters) of water at 195° F (90° C) for up to 5 7 infusions of 20-40 seconds each preceded by a quick rinse of the leaves.

Recommended with: apple pie, pastries, crème brûlée.

ORIENTAL BEAUTY

TYPE: WULONG TEA

AREA OF PROVENANCE: TAIWAN, NANTOU, AOWANDA

This 60% oxidized summer tea is grown in gardens at an altitude of about 4,595 feet (1,400 meters) in the region of Nantou. Oriental Beauty is a variety of Bai Hao which literally means "white tip," and is the most famous Wulong tea produced in Taiwan.

A certain event gives this tea its unique characteristics: the leaves are harvested in the summer only after small insects known as jassids have visited the gardens and nibbled the leaves. These insects are seen as angels sent from heaven, as their nibbling breaks the edges of the new leaves and starts a process of oxidation in the leaves that are still living and attached to branches. Once processed, the leaves turn red-brown with characteristic white tips. The flavor too is changed by the insects' work, which produces the typical delicate aroma of honey and peaches. This tea was formerly known as Formosa Wulong until Queen Elizabeth II, enchanted right from the first sip of this very special tea, renamed it Oriental Beauty.

TASTING NOTES
Dry: full-bodied, dark brown leaves with silvery shoots and fruity spicy notes.
Liquor: brilliant amber; fruity notes (fig, plum and cherry) in which peach dominates, alongside hints of honey, vanilla, spices (cinnamon and licorice) and wild orchid, with a lingering after taste.
Infusion: there are clear signs of insect bites on the leaves; the fruity, spicy notes linger, with a hint of woodiness.

PREPARATION
Western method: approx. 1/16 oz (2-3 grams) for every 2/3 cup (150 milliliters) of water at 195-205° F (90-95° C) for 5 minute infusion.
Eastern method: approx. 1/8 oz (5-6 grams) for every 2/3 cup (150 milliliters) of water at 195-205° F (90-95° C) for up to 6-7 infusions of 30-40 seconds each, preceded by a quick rinse of the leaves.

Recommended with: pulse soups, seasoned cheeses, spicy foods, pork, smoked fish, cold cuts.

BLUE-GREEN OR WULONG TEA

BERGAMOT WULONG

TYPE: SCENTED WULONG TEA
AREA OF PROVENANCE: TAIWAN, NANTOU, AOWANDA

Produced in the best gardens in the region of Nantou, Bergamot Wulong offers an exquisitely harmonious balance between the flowery and fruity notes of Wulongs from the high mountains and hints of citrus from fresh bergamot flowers. The delicate natural scent comes from blending the freshly processed tea leaves with the flowers of this plant. The result will win you over and leave you in doubt as to the value of the much over-hyped Earl Grey. This tea is 15% oxidized.

TASTING NOTES

Dry: dark green leaves with yellow tips, tightly rolled, with stalks and a small amount of bergamot zest.
Liquor: golden yellow, crystal clear; slightly astringent; the citrus and flower notes dominate with a delicate honeydew after taste.
Infusion: large dark green leaves with very thin pieces of bergamot peel.

PREPARATION

Western method: approx. 1/16 oz (2-3 grams) for every 2/3 cup (150 milliliters) of water at 185-195° F (85-90° C) for 5 minute infusion.
Eastern method: approx. 1/8 oz (5-6 grams) for every 2/3 cup (150 milliliters) of water at 185-195° F (85-90° C) for up to 5-7 infusions of 20-40 seconds each preceded by a quick rinse of the leaves.

Recommended with: shellfish, dark and white chocolate, lightly salted foods, carbohydrates and fruit.

BLUE-GREEN OR WULONG TEA

OSMANTHUS WULONG

TYPE: SCENTED WULONG TEA

AREA OF PROVENANCE: TAIWAN, NANTOU, AOWANDA

This delicate "nectar" comes from the region of Nantou, one of the best areas for the production of highly prized teas in the heart of Taiwan. It is processed with the very low oxidation factor of 12-15 % after having been harvested from plantations which sit 1400 meters above sea level. The delicate aroma of osmanthus flowers is very much appreciated in the East and is used to scent Wulong, green and red teas. This ever-green plant belongs to the Oleaceae family and has white-yellow flowers whose strong scent is reminiscent of magnolia, gardenia and freesia. The process, naturally transferring scent by contact, follows the same lines as that used for jasmine teas. Contact between the tea leaves and fresh flowers is repeated until the perfect balance between the fruity taste of Wulong and the flowery scent of osmanthus has been attained. Recommended for those who enjoy fresh Wulong and lightly oxidized teas.

TASTING NOTES

Dry: yellow-green, tightly rolled leaves.

Liquor: golden yellow, crystal clear; soft and velvety, with no astringent characteristics; the flowery top notes dominate, alongside delicate but lingering fruity base notes.

Infusion: large, light green leaves with dark red edges.

PREPARATION

Western method: approx. 1/16 oz (2-3 grams) for every 2/3 cup (150 milliliters) of water at 185-195° F (85-90° C) for 5 minute infusion.

Eastern method: approx. 1/8 oz (5-6 grams) for every 2/3 cup (150 milliliters) of water at 185-195° F (85-90° C) for up to 5-7 infusions of 20-40 seconds each, preceded by a quick rinse of the leaves.

Recommended with: fish and vegetable tempura, sweet and salty crêpes, fruit, white chocolate.

BLUE-GREEN OR WULONG TEA

The dual-chamber glass cups isolate heat, making it easier to enjoy teas requiring high infusion temperatures, like red teas.

RED TEA

According to the Chinese color classification, red teas are those commonly known as black teas in the West. The dark color of these teas, which led to their being called black by the British, is due to the high level of oxidation (not fermentation, as is often erroneously stated) to which the leaves are subjected during processing.

Withering, rolling, oxidation and drying are the basic stages of production.
During the first phase, the fresh leaves are spread out on racks and left to wither. This reduces their moisture by up to 60%, and makes them softer and easier to process, so that they do not break during subsequent manipulations. Rolling serves to release the leaves' essential oils and give them the desired shape.

At this point, a process of oxidation, performed through enzyme activity, "tints" the tea leaves red. This is the most important step in the processing of red tea. The leaves are spread out on racks to be air dried, thus obtaining their distinctive aroma and the typical color of oxidized tea. This red hue darkens further during the final drying phase, prior to storage, as the degree of hydration of the leaves reduces further.

Various classifications are used to indicate these completely oxidized teas.
In this book we will use the following criteria:

1. The term "red tea" will be used to refer to tea from China and Taiwan;
2. In line with the most widespread terminology, the term "black tea" will be used to refer to all the teas from other Asian countries: i.e. black Indian tea, black Sri Lankan tea, etc.

The dark red color typical of the liquor of oxidised teas is due to their particular production process.

CHINESE RED TEA

Chinese red tea is traditionally grown in the regions of Anhui, Yunnan and Fujian. The world renowned Qimen tea – a favorite with the British monarchy – comes from the city of Qimen, in the Anhui province. The well-informed report that this is the tea the Queen loves best, and is prepared for her birthday celebrations.

Qimen and Dian Hong, from the mountains of south-west Yunnan, without doubt share the title of best Chinese red teas. This region offers the ideal climatic and geological conditions for the cultivation of high quality teas. These red teas have complex bouquets, with perfectly balanced notes of flowers, cocoa, leather and cooked fruit.

Another famous tea, produced mainly for Western markets, is Zheng Shan Xiao Zhong, a smoked tea better known by the name of Lapsang Souchong. This tea, referred to by the Chinese as the "tea for Westerners," comes from the mountainous areas of WuYi Shan, in Fujian.

HOW TO PREPARE RED TEA

To prepare red teas, we recommend using porcelain, glass, or terracotta teapots. If you are a great admirer of red Yunnan or smoked teas, you should designate one terracotta teapot specifically to prepare teas in this family. The porousness of the terracotta, over the course of time, will continue to improve your tea set.

Use water that is between 195-205° F (90-95° C). According to your personal taste, you can do one 3-4 minute infusion or 4-5 brief infusions that are around 40 seconds each.

For either case, heat the teapot by filling it with boiling water. This water will be discarded before adding the tea leaves and proceeding to the infusion.

The ideal quantity is around 1/8 oz(6 grams, around one heaping tablespoon of tea leaves) for every 1 1/4 cups or 300 ml.

You do not have to briefly rinse the leaves before proceeding with the first infusion.

LAPSANG SOUCHONG - ZHENG SHAN XIAO ZHONG

TYPE: SCENTED RED TEA

AREA OF PROVENANCE: CHINA, FUJIAN, TONG MU

Zheng Shan Xiao Zhong (small leaf variety) is the real name of this very special red tea that is smoked with pine wood. More famous in the West than in its motherland, the original Lapsang Souchong comes from Tong Mu, a small village that sits amidst the WuYi Shan mountains in Fujian. Here, the Jiang family boasts of having created this special tea in the times of the Ming dynasty and of having produced it for more than 24 generations.

With its smoky taste, there is no in between: it is either loved by aficionados or hated for its very particular bitter taste. The smoky notes completely smother the aromas in the leaves. For this reason, it is produced using the Souchong, a very large leaf which has little aromatic content and a low level of tannin.

TASTING NOTES

Dry: the dark anthracite grey leaves have very intense empyreumatic notes (bacon).
Liquor: amber in color, it is a strong tea with very noticeable smoky notes that linger on the palate.
Infusion: the leaves are brown tending to beige.

PREPARATION

Approx. 1/16 oz (2-3 grams) for every 2/3 cup (150 milliliters) of water at 205° F (95° C) for 3 minute infusion.

Recommended with: perfect with brunch, large fish (tuna, cod), game, flavored cheeses, eggs, or used as a "spice" instead of pancetta in vegetarian recipes.

RED TEA

QIMEN

TYPE: RED TEA

AREA OF PROVENANCE: CHINA, ANHUI, QIMEN

Produced in Qimen in the Anhui region, for many years this was considered the best Chinese red tea. Qimen (English transliteration of Keemun) is a strong tea with a rich aromatic liquor and a delicate scent of orchids. Production only began fairly recently.

In 1876, a retired high functionary from this area, known for the excellence of its tea, introduced the red tea processing technique he had learned while working in Fujian. The result was a great success: this really is the Queen of all teas. While on the subject, well-informed sources say that this tea is a favorite at Buckingham Palace.

TASTING NOTES

Dry: thin, dark, stubby leaves with a few golden shoots.

Liquor: brilliant red with aromatic fruity notes and a lingering flavor of orchids; soft and velvety, with no astringent characteristics.

Infusion: the dark red leaves have a scent of cooked fruit, leather and cocoa.

PREPARATION

Approx. 1/16 oz (2-3 grams) for every 2/3 cup (150 milliliters) of water at 195-205° F (90-95° C) for 3 minute infusion.

Recommended with: red meat, soft cheeses (Reblochon, Camembert, Gorgonzola), eggs and pizza.

GOLDEN YUNNAN

TYPE: RED TEA

AREA OF PROVENANCE: CHINA, YUNNAN, LING YUN

This red tea is made exclusively from golden shoots (from whence it takes its name) from the mountain plantations in the Ling Yun reserve, in the region of Yunnan. This is considered the best Dian Hong from the area. The word Dian is an abbreviation of the name Yunnan while Hong is the Chinese word for red, the color of oxidized teas. The plant variety and a special oxidization process turn the leaves a unique red color which, in the cup, transforms into a delicate fruity, flowery aroma that is typical of the most prized red teas of Yunnan.

A sophisticated tea for breakfast or any other time of day.

TASTING NOTES

Dry: the harvest consists of gathering long golden tipped shoots covered with a light coat of feathery down.
Liquor: amber-red with a complex yet unique bouquet of harmoniously balanced fruity, flowery and honeyed notes, with a hint of woodiness.
Infusion: the leaves are a brilliant red-brown in color and well proportioned.

PREPARATION

Western method: approx. 1/16 oz (2-3 grams) for every 2/3 cup (150 milliliters) of water at 195° F (90° C) for 2-3 minute infusion.
Eastern method: 1/8 oz (5 grams) for every 2/3 cup (150 milliliters) of water at 195° F (90° C) for up to 4 infusions of 20-40 seconds each.

Recommended with: perfect with a continental breakfast, lightly salted foods, grilled meats, lamb, almond desserts, milk or white chocolate, fruit compotes and pizza.

RED MAO FENG

TYPE: RED TEA

AREA OF PROVENANCE: CHINA, YUNNAN, LINCANG

Red Mao Feng is one of the most highly prized teas belonging to the Dian Hong category, and is the archetypal Yunnan red tea. This variety consists exclusively of golden shoots with a light down covering, and comes from the mountain plantations in the region of Licang at 3,280 feet (1,000 meters) above sea level.
After preparation, the liquor is bright red with a sweet taste and a delicate aroma.

A fantastic tea for any time of day.

TASTING NOTES

Dry: curly golden leaves.
Liquor: a lively and brilliant dark red in the cup; it releases a delicate flowery, fruity scent and a lingering flavor; as well as the mature fruit notes, there are hints of malt and cocoa; delicate but with character.
Infusion: the steeped leaves take on a brilliant red-brown hue.

PREPARATION

Western method: approx. 1/16oz (2-3 grams) for every 2/3 cup (150 milliliters) of water at 205° F (90° C) for 2-3 minute infusion.
Eastern method: 1/8 oz (5 grams) for every 2/3 cup (150 milliliters) of water at 205° F (90° C) for up to 4 infusions of 20-40 seconds each.

Recommended with: perfect with a continental breakfast, grilled meats, game, smoked fish, almond desserts, milk or white chocolate, fruit compotes and apple pie.

INDIAN AND SRI LANKAN BLACK TEA

Tea was first produced in India in the nineteenth century. The British had studied the possibility of growing tea in their colony using seeds from China. However, their complete ignorance in the matter and the lack of long-standing know-how meant that the project was a complete failure. Robert Bruce also made failed attempts in Assam to grow a local plant similar to the tea the English had observed in China. The first crop, sold in Calcutta in 1836, was of very poor quality. At this point, there was only one possible solution: the British Crown sent a botanist named Robert Fortune to China on an espionage mission with the purpose of stealing plants, seeds, and, above all, the secrets behind cultivating tea on a large scale.

In the second half of the 1800s, production expanded from Assam, to Nilgiri and Darjeeling, close to the Himalayas. Within a few decades, the volume of Indian tea imported into England became higher than that from China. The black teas produced in India are not intended solely for exportation, but also for local consumption, where the traditional "chai" is drunk on a daily basis. This is a fragrant mixture of black teas, spices, sugar and milk. The four annual harvests – in spring (March and April), summer (May and June), monsoon time (July-August) and autumn (October and November) – each offer different aromatic notes. The harvests most sought after by connoisseurs are those of spring (first flush) and summer (second flush). First flush harvests provide light, slight astringent teas with a flowery fragrance and hints of nutmeg and green almonds. Second flush harvests have a fruity nutmeg flavor. They are smoother, more rounded and full-bodied than spring teas.

In the nineteenth century, coffee was extensively cultivated in Sri Lanka. Following a disaster caused by a parasite, tea cultivation gradually replaced coffee, soon making Ceylon the world's second largest producer of tea worldwide. The main areas of production are: Galle, Kandy, Nuwara Eliya, Ratnapura, Dimbula and Uva. Teas are not only classified by area of origin, but also by plantation altitude: therefore, we have high grown teas (3,937 feet - above 1,200 meters), mid grown teas (between 1,970 and 3,937 feet - between 600 and 1,200 meters) and low grown teas (below 1,970 feet - below 600 meters).

HOW TO PREPARE BLACK TEA:
ENGLISH TEA

The rules for the art of preparing English tea are the following:

1. choose a mild water, spring or fixed dry residue, and heat it to 195-205° F (90-95° C);

2. warm the teapot by pouring hot water inside. Wait a few moments, then discard the water;

3. add one teaspoon of tea leaves for each cup, plus one for the pot.

4. Add the heated water and wait around 2-3 minutes for first flush Darjeeling, and 3 minutes for other Indian or Singhalese teas;

5. filter and serve in white porcelain cups.

The perfect tea time must be accompanied by scones, clotted cream, strawberry jam, tea sandwiches, cakes, and pastries.

The English love to drink tea with milk and one or two cubes of sugar.

DARJEELING CASTLETON FTGFOP1 - SF

TYPE: BLACK TEA

AREA OF PROVENANCE: INDIA, DARJEELING, CASTLETON

This is the classic breakfast tea, and the proud holder of the title of "Wonder Muscatel," which characterizes the high quality Darjeeling summer teas, with their rare fruity aroma. The bite of an insect known as jassid sets off the oxidization process in the leaves before they are even harvested, creating the typical fruity notes of this summer tea. Darjeeling Muscatel are very much loved for their elegant aroma and rounded, harmonious liquor. This garden in the northern Kurseong region grows at an altitude of between 3,281 and 6,562 feet (1,000 and 2,000 meters) and is one of the most famous and prized in the Darjeeling area. Muscatel is a "historical" Indian tea whose production began in the late 19th century.

TASTING NOTES

Dry: the leaves are a dark hazelnut color with golden tips created by the presence of shoots.
Liquor: dark orange with shades of gold; soft, enveloping with fruity (grapes, plums, citrus fruits), flowery and woody notes.
Infusion: even and brilliant dark leather color; the fruity, flowery, woody notes tend to linger in the mouth.

PREPARATION

Approx. 1/16 oz (2-3 grams) for every 2/3 cup (150 milliliters) of water at 195° F (90° C) for 3 minutes.

Recommended with: ideal with a continental breakfast, gnocchi or stuffed pasta, lemon chicken, mushroom quiche, sweet and salty crêpes, orange curd pastries, apple pie and honey sweets.

DARJEELING GOPALDHARA FTGFOP1 - FF

TYPE: BLACK TEA

AREA OF PROVENANCE: INDIA, DARJEELING, GOPALDHARA

The gardens of Gopaldhara flourish in the Mirik valley at an altitude of between 5,577 and 7,218 feet (1,700 and 2,200 meters). Gopaldhara is the highest tea plantation in Darjeeling and the second highest in the world. The rigid climate at high altitude means that the harvest is 4-5 weeks later than is usual. The cold also affects the taste, which is more delicate than that of teas harvested at normal altitudes.

TASTING NOTES

Dry: large dark green leaves, tightly rolled with silvery buds; fruity and flowery notes with a lightly toasted underlying aroma.

Liquor: slightly astringent with a brilliant copper color; a flowery bouquet followed by notes of citrus fruits, almonds and vanilla guarantee a unique infusion: a classic tea that wins over all who try it.

Infusion: the leaves are mainly green with a few brown shades.

PREPARATION

Approx. 1/16 oz (2-3 grams) for every 2/3 cup (150 milliliters) of water at 185-195° F (85-90° C) for 3 minute infusion.

Recommended with: with their notes of tannin, Darjeeling teas are perfect with a continental breakfast and with carbohydrates. Also perfect with grilled fish, salmon, cheeses (such as brie, mozzarella and camembert), lamb, eggs and fresh fruit.

DARJEELING JUNGPANA FTGFOP1 - SF
WONDER MUSCATEL

TYPE: BLACK TEA

AREA OF PROVENANCE: INDIA, DARJEELING, JUNGPANA

Hidden in the heart of the Himalayas, the Jungpana garden is known the world over for its tea with a characteristic aroma of nutmeg. High quality tea has been produced here for more than a century. The name "Wonder Muscatel" indicates the typical fruity bouquet of nutmeg that characterizes several Darjeeling summer teas. As occurs with the Bai Hao Wulong tea from Taiwan, during the summer insects known as jassids nibble at the plant's tender leaves, changing their chemical composition. During the oxidization phase, these very bites give rise to particularly fruity and woody notes. The plantation which lies near the city of Darjeeling enjoys a privileged south-facing position at an altitude of between 3,281 and 4,593 feet (1,000 and 1,400 meters). The gardens, however, are difficult to reach, and to this day, village men carry the tea downhill in wooden crates. Tea made from the second Jungpana harvest is a real treat in the morning, with or without milk. Its softness on the palate is reminiscent of the best Wulong teas.

TASTING NOTES

Dry: the leaves are dark hazelnut in color.

Liquor: orange with shades of gold. Soft, enveloping with fruity (grapes, plums), flowery and woody notes.

Infusion: color of dark leather; lingering flowery, fruity and slightly spicy notes.

PREPARATION

Approx. 1/16 oz (2-3 grams) for every 2/3 cup (150 milliliters) of water at 195° F (90° C) for 3 minute infusion.

Recommended with: ideal with a continental breakfast, with honey sweets, sweet and salty crêpes, and orange curd pastries.

DARJEELING MARGARET'S HOPE FTGFOP1 - FF

TYPE: BLACK TEA

AREA OF PROVENANCE: INDIA, DARJEELING, MARGARET'S HOPE

The peaks of the Himalayas rise in the background in one of the most beautiful landscapes in the Darjeeling region. This is where the Margaret's Hope plantation lies.

Apart from its natural beauty, this tea producing area is also well known for its "champagne" quality black tea, rooted in a tradition that dates back to 1860.

An abundance of dense rain forests, wild orchids and velvet moss create the ideal environment for the cultivation of tea in complete harmony with the ecosystem.

This tea is a first flush variety with soft, beautifully variegated leaves, bearing witness to the sophisticated style of this garden. The tea offers a rare flowery taste with pleasant almond notes.

TASTING NOTES

Dry: brilliant slightly rounded green leaves with silver tips provided by small shoots; intense, fresh flowery notes with a delicate fruity scent and hints of "confiserie."

Liquor: yellow/gold with shades of amber; slightly astringent to the palate with a rounded, long lasting, velvety flavor; fresh flowery top notes are followed by hints of ripe fruits, nuts (almonds) and spices.

Infusion: mixed color but mainly brilliant green with brown and red tips; the flowery notes and nut flavor linger in the mouth.

PREPARATION

Approx. 1/16 oz (2-3 grams) for every 2/3 cup (150 milliliters) of water at 185° F (85° C) for 2-3 minute infusion.

Recommended with: thanks to its tannin notes, this tea is perfect with carbohydrates, savory quiches, eggs, cold cuts, lamb, game, marinated and smoked fish, and chocolate.

DARJEELING SEEYOK FTGFOP1 - FF

TYPE: BLACK TEA

AREA OF PROVENANCE: INDIA, DARJEELING, SEEYOK

This is an organically produced first flush tea from the plantations of Seeyok, an uncontaminated area in the Mirik Valley sitting at an altitude of 3,610 - 5,905 feet (1,100 to 1,800 meters) above sea level.
This area, astride the India-Nepal border, is protected by the Kanchenjunga mountain chain, which provides one of the most stunning landscapes in the Himalayas. The cultivation of tea, which began in 1869, has recently shifted to organic growing methods, and affects an area measuring more than 370 acres (150 hectares).

The fog, the cold sharp mountain air, the rains and the intermittent sun, contribute to the merits of this classic tea, which is protected by a Designation of Origin. It is a tea for drinking at breakfast time or in the afternoon, and is best with neither milk, lemon nor sugar.

TASTING NOTES

Dry: large very green leaves with a splash of silver and hazelnut brown.
Liquor: golden yellow, slightly astringent and with the taste of flowers, vanilla and almond typical of Darjeeling first flush that satisfies the senses.
Infusion: the leaves are light green with hazelnut brown tips; the fragrance of flowers with light empyreumatic notes is even more intense.

PREPARATION

Approx. 1/16 oz (2-3 grams) for every 2/3 cup (150 milliliters) of water at 185° F (85° C) for 2-3 minute infusion.

Recommended with: thanks to its elegant tannic notes, this tea is perfect with a continental breakfast, carbohydrates, quiche, salmon, lamb and chocolate.

BLACK TEA

ASSAM HATTIALLI FTGFOP1 - SF

TYPE: BLACK TEA

AREA OF PROVENANCE: INDIA, ASSAM, HATTIALLI

The garden's name comes from Hatti Alli which means "road of the elephants."

Thanks to its position and the favorable climate it enjoys, Hattialli can provide high quality harvests all year round.

This tea is recommended for those looking for a classic black Indian tea with a rich full-bodied taste.

It is a superb morning tea and is also perfect with a dash of milk.

TASTING NOTES

Dry: regular, large leaves with a high proportion of golden shoots.

Liquor: dark, amber colored and full-bodied; a perfect balance of aromatic spicy, malty, fruity, cocoa notes; full-bodied with a lingering flavor, this is beyond any doubt the best tea from Assam.

Infusion: the color is between dark green, red and brown.

PREPARATION

Approx. 1/16 oz (2-3 grams) for every 2/3 cup (150 milliliters) of water at 195° F (90° C) for 3 minute infusion.

Recommended with: ideal with a continental or English breakfast, roast meats and mushrooms.

ASSAM BANASPATY FTGFOP1 - FF

TYPE: BLACK TEA
AREA OF PROVENANCE: INDIA, ASSAM, BANASPATY

Teas from the Banaspaty gardens offer everything you'd expect from a quality Assam: a strong tea which is perfect for breakfast, with its characteristic malty aroma.

The first harvest has a rich taste and full-bodied aroma. First flush Assams, despite their worth, are little known in Europe. The second flush varieties however are more commonly found and are often used in the preparation of blends. This is one of the ingredients used in blending Earl Grey.

TASTING NOTES

Leaf: regular dark brown leaves with golden shoots.
Liquor: amber in color, enticing the palate with its slightly spicy notes and malty, woody aroma; full-bodied, lingering flavor.
Infusion: the leaves are dark, with aromatic fruity, woody, malty notes.

PREPARATION

Approx. 1/16 oz (2-3 grams) for every 2/3 cup (150 milliliters) of water at 195° F (90° C) for 3 minute infusion.

Recommended with: the malty notes contrast softly with salmon. Delicious with a continental breakfast, red meats and dark chocolate.

*Indian Assam black tea, with its characteristic malty flavour and amber colour,
is the breakfast tea par excellence.*

NUWARA ELIYA HIGH GROWN

TYPE: BLACK TEA

AREA OF PROVENANCE: SRI LANKA, NUWARA ELIYA

Teas of the High Grown variety (3,937-5,905 feet - 1,200-1,800 meters) from the Nuwara Eliya region are very delicate and can be compared with French Champagne in terms of fame. The high altitudes and cold weather all year round mean tea plants grow very slowly and with unusually small leaves that take on an orange hue after drying. Other factors adding to their special taste are the wild mint, eucalyptus and cypress that grow alongside the plantation.

TASTING NOTES

Dry: the leaves are average sized, with the occasional long one, and at times – something quite unusual in this region – they have a greenish color.
Liquor: the golden orange color is slightly paler than in other varieties of teas produced in Sri Lanka; light and delicate but with character, the tea can also be served iced in summer.
Infusion: the dark green leaves tend towards copper.

PREPARATION

Approx. 1/16 oz (2-3 grams) for every 2/3 cup (150 milliliters) of water at 195-205° F (90-95° C) for 3 minute infusion.

Recommended with: continental breakfast (bread, jam, cheese), English breakfast (fried eggs, bacon fried bread), lightly salted foods, cheeses (e.g.: Provolone), and honey sweets.

BLACK TEA

RUHUNA GOLDEN TIPS

TYPE: BLACK TEA
AREA OF PROVENANCE: SRI LANKA, RUHUNA, MATARA DISTRICT

This tea took its name from the ancient Ceylonese word for the southern region of the island and is considered the pearl of Sri Lanka. Ruhuna teas are "low-grown" teas and are cultivated at altitudes of between 1,970 feet (600 meters) and sea level. Ruhuna Golden Tips is made exclusively from the plant's carefully selected long golden shoots. It is produced in very limited quantities and is of extremely high quality. Unlike other black teas, Golden Tips is only slightly oxidized. It comes from particularly fertile plantations which sit near the Sinharaja rain forest, where the combination of humidity, rainfall and special earth bless Golden Tips with an extraordinary and unique scent.

TASTING NOTES

Dry: long golden shoots encased with a soft down.

Liquor: amber-orange, fresh and delicate scent with notes of flowers, fruit and honey.

Infusion: perfectly regular and hazelnut in color; lingering flowery notes with hints of leather and a spicy top note.

PREPARATION

Approx. 1/8 oz (3-5 grams) for every 2/3 cup (150 milliliters) of water at 195° F (90° C) for 3 minute infusion.

Recommended with: perfect with a continental breakfast, lightly salted foods, mushrooms, vegetables, fish, fruit pies.

UVA HIGH GROWN

TYPE: BLACK TEA

AREA OF PROVENANCE: SRI LANKA, UVA

This is one of the teas from the Uva region that lies to the east of Nuwara Eliya and Dimbula, on the central plateau of the island, at an altitude of over 3,937 feet (1,200 meters). Experts attribute the unique character of this tea to the local climate. The region is exposed to winds from both the north-east and the south-west, and even thought there are monsoons, the climate is relatively dry. This is because the surrounding mountains feature numerous clefts that channel the rains from the monsoons to the lower hillsides. The "dry" monsoons interrupt the normal process of photosynthesis of the tea plants, while the very hot days and cold nights bring about chemical changes which improve the taste of this tea.

TASTING NOTES

Dry: the fairly long, curly leaves are nearly black with occasional spots of brown.
Liquor: dark brown; a sweet tea with an astringent, slightly minty taste with exotic notes of wood and spices; it is often used in blends, and is best drunk pure.
Infusion: the dark brown leaves tend towards copper.

PREPARATION

Approx. 1/16 oz (2-3 grams) for every 2/3 cup (150 milliliters) of water at 195-205° F (90 -95° C) for 3 minute infusion.

Recommended with: continental breakfast (bread, jam, cheese), English breakfast (fried tomatoes, fried bread, eggs, bacon), mushroom risotto, couscous made with vegetables and white meats, pizza, salamis and capers.

BLACK TEA

FERMENTED (OR BLACK) TEA

The most famous black tea is Pu'er, which term denotes a very large family of teas including several loose-leaf and compressed varieties, the latter formed into the shape of bricks, cakes, nests or melons. This tea is produced using a wide-leaf botanical specimen known as Da Ye, which grows in the southern part of Yunnan, on the border with Laos and Myanmar. Moreover, in order to be defined as Pu'er, the leaves must have been dried in the sun and must have undergone either natural or controlled fermentation. Pu'ers are currently classified as black teas, but in recent years Chinese experts have been debating whether to create a new tea category for them, or keep them in the macro-family of fermented teas also produced outside Yunnan.

These Chinese black teas are produced in the regions of Yunnan, Hunan, Sichuan, Hubei and Guangxi. Chinese black tea is also known as Bianxiao Cha, or "border-sale tea" because it was mainly consumed by frontier populations. As travel was difficult in these mountainous regions, the tea was historically transported on horseback to Tibet, Hong Kong and Macao. For years, the Tea-Horse Road brought into contact different cultures, nationalities and religions, spreading the tea tradition worldwide.

The leaves of this type of tea undergo a process of veritable fermentation. From a chemical point of view, fermentation is very different to oxidation, and is carried out by micro-organisms present on the tea leaves rather than contact with oxygen.

These are the only teas to be fermented, and also the only ones that need to be seasoned before being sold, as only time can enhance their characteristic scent.

Moreover, the most valuable varieties are not consumed immediately, but are set aside for ageing.

The processing procedure initially involves heating the tea leaves on high heat, to stop oxidation and enzyme activity. Next, the leaves are rolled to release their essential oils and give them their shape. The leaves are then dried in the sun until they lose 90% of their water content. At this point, they are ready to be stacked in regular piles and sprayed with water. This sets off the natural fermentation process.

During the final drying stage, the leaves are scattered to be air dried, thus releasing any residual moisture.

The healing properties of these "medicinal teas" have been appreciated in China ever since the Tang era.

Since the 1970s, many Western scientific studies have also recognized their power to aid digestion, significantly lower the level of bad cholesterol in the blood, and reduce the absorption of fat and sugar, making these teas veritable allies in slimming diets. Basically, drinking 3 cups of fermented tea a day is like treating yourself to sips of health.

This spoutless teapot, in porcelain with blue decorations, enables the infusion to be repeated up to 10-12 times, and enhances the undergrowth aroma typical of Pu'er black. teas.

HOW TO PREPARE FERMENTED TEA

To prepare fermented Chinese teas, we recommend using a white porcelain or Yi Xing terra-cotta teapot. In China, there are sets for this purpose, made out of white or decorated porcelain, that consist of a spoutless teapot and teacups that are wider in diameter compared to those used to drink other types of tea.

In order to correctly prepare fermented tea, we recommend you follow these instructions:
1. Place the teapot, jug and teacups on the ceremonial table with the special tray to catch any liquids;
2. After heating the water to 205° F (95° C), pour it into the teapot, jug and teacups to heat and rinse the tea set.
3. Pour out the water and place tea leaves into the teapot (around 5-6 g for every 2/3 of a cup or 150 ml). If the tea is compressed, remove the desired quantity from the brick with a special knife. It is preferable to infuse small pieces, because if the portion of Pu'er cake is too large and compact, an ideal infusion will not be achieved.
4. Pour the water over the leaves or the portion of compressed brick and briefly rinse the tea.
5. Discard the rinse water and start with the infusion. After around 1 minute, stop the infusion by pouring all of the tea into the jar, and then serve it in the teacups.

With the Chinese Gong Fu Cha method, fermented black teas can withstand around 10-12 infusions of 1 minute each.
If instead you prefer to use the European preparation method, one 4-5 minute infusion can be performed with a quantity of 2-3 g of tea leaves for every 2/3 of a cup (150 ml).

Pu'er black tea "cake." The portion of leaves required for the infusion is cut off horizontally, to avoid crushing the tea leaves, using a special knife for cutting compressed teas.

FERMENTED (OR BLACK) TEA

PU'ER SHENG CHA - CAKE

TYPE: FERMENTED TEA
AREA OF PROVENANCE: CHINA, YUNNAN, LIN CANG

Pu'er green tea (defined as raw or "not cooked" tea) initially undergoes a processing procedure which is similar to that used for green teas. After harvesting, Pu'er leaves are traditionally dried in the sun, one of the characteristics that make the processing of these teas so unique.

If weather conditions are unfavorable or if drying needs to be speeded up, the leaves are placed in ovens, though it must be said, this does affect quality. Given the growing popularity of Pu'er teas, producers can be increasingly tempted to speed up the process using artificial methods, so great care must be taken. In the traditional process, ovens are only used to heat the cakes once the leaves have been compressed, to remove residual moisture and to prevent the formation of moulds. The end result is an aromatic, complex liquor.

Apart from the cake shape, Pu'er Sheng Cha teas can also come in many different sizes and forms, for example in the form of a small nest (tuo cha or mini tuo cha), a square or rectangular brick, a melon, or even just as tea leaves.

Fresh Sheng Cha cakes can have an astringent taste with a slightly bitter note. Fresh with a lingering flavor, this tea undergoes a "refinement" phase but. With the passing of time, the taste improves and the tea releases more complex aromatic notes. It is fascinating to sample it as time goes by. Once matured, the quality is often better than that of Shu Cha Pu'er teas.

TASTING NOTES

Dry: the tea cakes are grey-green in color with the shoots visible on the surface.

Liquor: dull dark yellow; the herbal taste is slightly bitter, sometimes with animal notes that disappear during the natural ageing process.

Infusion: the leaves are khaki green.

PREPARATION

Western method: approx. 1/16 oz (2-3 grams) for every 2/3 cup (150 milliliters) of water at 205° F (95° C) for 4 minutes.

Eastern method: 1/8 oz (5 grams) for every 2/3 cup (150 milliliters) of water at 205° F (95° C) for up to 10 infusions of 1 minute each, preceded by a quick rinse of the leaves.

Recommended with: first course vegetable based dishes and fish-based second courses.

FERMENTED (OR BLACK) TEA

PU'ER SHU CHA - CAKE

TYPE: FERMENTED TEA

AREA OF PROVENANCE: CHINA, YUNNAN, LINCANG

Red Pu'er tea (defined as cooked) undergoes a processing procedure similar to that used for green Pu'er Sheng Cha teas, plus a secret post-fermentation process which serves to speed up the ageing process and to imitate the flavor of an aged Sheng Cha tea.

During this second fermentation, the leaves are left under special impermeable sheets for 40-60 days.

Unlike green Pu'er Sheng Cha which "refines" with the passing of the years, Pu'er Shu Cha can be drunk immediately.

Pu'er Shu Cha teas are a recent innovation, as this technique was only introduced in the early 70s to cope with increased demand. This period set a clear line of demarcation in the history of fermented teas. All Pu'er teas processed before this date were authentic and fermented naturally, without any need for a chemical reaction introduced by man.

TASTING NOTES

Dry: the chocolate colored cakes have slightly lighter golden shoots on the surface.

Liquor: very dark amber, brilliant and crystal clear; the scent is reminiscent of wood, mushrooms and forest earth; the sweet, delicate and delicious flavor lingers persistently on the palate.

Infusion: black leaves with intense notes of musk, wet earth and wood

PREPARATION

Western method: approx. 1/16 oz (2-3 grams) for every 2/3 cup (150 milliliters) of water at 205° F (95° C) for 4 minute infusion.

Eastern method: 1/8 oz (5 grams) for every 2/3 cup (150 milliliters) of water at 205° F (95° C) for up to 10-12 infusions of 1 minute each, preceded by a quick rinse of the leaves.

Recommended with: eggs, seasoned cheeses, red meats, cold cuts and mushrooms.

FERMENTED (OR BLACK) TEA

PU'ER STEMS - BRICK

TYPE: FERMENTED TEA

AREA OF PROVENANCE: CHINA, YUNNAN, SIMAO

This very unusual compressed, fermented Pu'er is a specialty of Simao, one of the oldest tea production areas in Chinese history. Ancient wild tea plants with long stems grow amidst the mountains sitting to the extreme south of Yunnan. This unique black tea is produced using their tender branches. Unlike the leaves, the branches are the part of the plant that are richest in amino acids, which are vital to the process of cell renovation. Much softer and more delicate than other Pu'er teas, this variety is recommended for those who want to better appreciate the forest scents that are so typical of this family of tea. With its extremely low tannin content, this tea is ideal at any time of day.

TASTING NOTES

Dry: the brick of tea branches is chocolate in color.

Liquor: very dark amber, almost black; the scent is reminiscent of wood and wet forest earth; soft, delicate and delicious on the palate.

Infusion: black leaves with an intense scent of musk, wet earth and wood.

PREPARATION

Western method: approx. 1/16 oz (2-3 grams) for every 2/3 cup (150 milliliters) of water at 205° F (95° C) for 4 minute infusion.

Eastern method: 1/8 oz (5 grams) for every 2/3 cup (150 milliliters) of water at 205° F (95° C) for up to 10-12 infusions of 1 minute each, preceded by a quick rinse of the leaves.

Recommended with: eggs, seasoned cheeses, red meats, cold cuts and mushrooms.

FERMENTED (OR BLACK) TEA

FU CHA TOP GRADE - BRICK

TYPE: FERMENTED TEA
AREA OF PROVENANCE: CHINA, HUNAN, AN HUA

Hunan black tea: a classic and one of the best known Chinese black teas. This tea has been used for hundreds of years in traditional Chinese medicine for treating digestive problems, in weight loss diets, for its anti-arrhythmic effects on the heart, for reducing cholesterol and for its anti-bacterial properties. Fermented Fu Cha tea is rich in intestinal flora, which act on the body as a natural antibiotic. Although not well known in the West, its plays an important role in the high protein diet of the people of Tibet, Mongolia and North West of China. It is an excellent source of minerals and vitamins, and is effective in controlling the levels of sugars and fats in the bloodstream. Thanks to its nutritional properties, it can supplement a diet in which fruit and vegetables are not plentiful. The original name of Hu Cha was changed to Fu Cha, as this tea is compressed during the period known as Fu, i.e. the hottest days of the summer. It differs from Pu'er in that during the second phase of fermentation, a beneficial fungus known as "Golden Flower" (Eurotium Cristatum) forms. The amount of fungus affects the quality of Fu Cha: the more fungus there is, the higher the quality.

TASTING NOTES

Dry: very dark leaves compressed to form bricks.

Liquor: orange-amber, sweet and not astringent, with aromatic flowery, woody notes; with a high quality sample, the taste lingers persistently on the palate.

Infusion: very dark anthracite grey leaves tending to black.

PREPARATION

Eastern method: 1/8 oz (5 grams) for every 2/3 cup (150 milliliters) of water at 205° F (95° C) for up to 10-12 infusions of 60 seconds each, preceded by a quick rinse of the leaves.

Recommended with: pulse soups, red meats, seasoned cheeses, or after meals to stimulate digestion.

FERMENTED (OR BLACK) TEA

183

PROCESSED TEAS

SCENTED, FLAVORED, AND BLOOMING TEAS

As we saw earlier, Chinese teas are divided into six macro-families, split by color classification, depending on how the tea leaves are processed after harvest.

Once the basic processing, which is different for each tea category, is complete, the finished, or "pure" product is ready to be sold. In some cases, however, these same teas may be further treated to produce the so-called "processed teas."

This macro-category includes scented, flavored and blooming teas.

The art of "scenting" and "flavoring" tea leaves is an ancient Chinese tradition applied to any kind of "pure" tea. Scented tea is produced mainly in the regions of Guangxi, Fujian, Sichuan and Yunnan.

In scented teas, processed tea leaves are place in contact with fresh flowers, such as jasmine, gardenia, orange blossom, sweet osmanthus and roses.

Once the flowers have released their delicate scent, they are removed from the tea leaves. For aesthetic reasons, a few flowers are left, even once the scenting process is complete.

Naturally, scented teas are much more delicate than flavored teas, which obtain their aroma, not through contact with fresh flowers, but through the addition of natural or artificial flavorings reminiscent of flowers, fruits, spices, and so on.

Blooming teas also belong to the macro-category of processed "pure" teas. In this case, tea shoots and flowers are tied together in striking bundles, such as spheres, mushrooms, towers, and even Buddhas. These give the liquor a delicate floral aroma while providing an experience of great visual impact.

Regarded as meditation teas, refined "blooming teas" offer the beautiful sight
of a flower unfurling – a real delight for the eye as much as for the palate.

20 RECIPES

BY CHEF GIOVANNI RUGGIERI

TEA TIME
AND SERVING
SUGGESTIONS

Tea is the second most popular drink in the world, after water, enjoyed just about at any time of day. It is difficult to identify a particular time for tea, as in fact any occasion is suitable for experimenting new pairings with both sweet and savory foods.

Tea is ideal during a meal, as it "cleanses" the mouth and enhances the flavor of food. This is partly because it is usually consumed hot, and heat highlights our perception of taste.

The pairing between tea and food is generally dictated by personal taste, and there are no hard and fast rules in this regard. However, by following a number of basic guidelines, it is possible to harmoniously match the distinctive flavors of each food with the most suitable tea.

Trial and practice lead to the detection of an ideal equilibrium, offering new pleasant sensorial experiences. Elements of taste must enhance, rather than dominate or cover one another. The point is to find a delicate sensory balance, based either on similarity or contrast. The latter are the most difficult pairings, but at the same time the most original and successful. In this case, the tea has to create an experience on the palate that is different to that brought about by the food: if the dish is fat and oily, the tea must be fresh and mildly astringent; sweetmeats must be toned down by a full-bodied, slightly bitter tea; strong or smoky flavors must be matched with delicate teas. Moreover, when tea is used as an ingredient of a dish, it should also be served hot alongside that dish.

Sugar, honey and creamy desserts are often enhanced by sweet teas with floral or fruity notes.

THE MOST COMMON PAIRINGS ARE:

- LIGHT SALTED FOOD: CHINESE GREEN TEAS, WULONG TEAS, INDIAN BLACK TEAS
- CARBOHYDRATES: INDIAN OR SRI LANKAN BLACK TEAS, WULONG TEAS, GREEN TEAS
- VEGETABLES: WULONG TEAS, CHINESE AND JAPANESE GREEN TEAS
- EGGS: FERMENTED TEAS, SMOKED TEAS
- FISH: CHINESE AND JAPANESE GREEN TEAS, WHITE TEAS
- MOLLUSKS: JAPANESE GREEN TEAS
- WHITE MEAT: CHINESE AND JAPANESE GREEN TEAS, WHITE TEAS, YELLOW TEAS, INDIAN BLACK TEAS
- RED MEAT: SMOKED TEAS, CHINESE RED TEAS, INDIAN BLACK TEAS
- SMOKED FLAVORS: INDIAN BLACK TEAS, WULONG TEAS
- SHELLFISH: BERGAMOT-FLAVORED WULONG TEAS, CHINESE GREEN TEAS
- FRESH CHEESE: CHINESE AND JAPANESE GREEN TEAS, JASMINE PEARL TEAS
- BLUE CHEESE: JASMINE PEARL TEAS, WHITE TEAS, CHINESE RED TEAS
- MATURE CHEESE: SMOKED TEAS
- SPICY FOOD: JASMINE PEARL GREEN TEAS, CHINESE GREEN TEAS, WULONG TEAS
- DARK CHOCOLATE: INDIAN BLACK TEAS, BERGAMOT WULONG TEAS
- MILK OR WHITE CHOCOLATE: WULONG TEAS
- MUSHROOMS: FERMENTED TEAS, INDIAN OR SRI LANKAN BLACK TEAS
- FRUIT: CHINESE GREEN TEAS, WULONG TEAS, INDIAN BLACK TEAS
- NUTS: YELLOW TEAS
- PASTRIES: INDIAN BLACK TEAS, YELLOW TEAS

RED SHRIMP CRUDO WITH MATCHA GREEN MAYONNAISE AND SPROUTS

4 SERVINGS

FOR THE SHRIMP

12 SICILIAN RED SHRIMP, HEADS AND SHELLS REMOVED
OIL, AS NEEDED
SALT FLAKES, AS NEEDED
A FEW DROPS OF LEMON JUICE

FOR THE MAYONNAISE

1 EGG YOLK
1/16 OZ (2 G) SALT
10 DROPS LEMON JUICE
2/3 CUP (150 ML) EXTRA VIRGIN OLIVE OIL
1/4 OZ (10 G) MATCHA

FOR PLATING

SOME RADISH, TURNIP, AND GREEN SHISO SPROUTS
A FEW EDIBLE GERBER DAISY PETALS

PREPARATION

Freeze the shrimp for 12 hours. Once they have been defrosted (it is important that they are defrosted at room temperature), season them with a bit of oil, salt flakes, and a few drops of lemon juice.

To prepare the mayonnaise, beat the egg yolk with the salt and lemon juice. Once the components are well blended, add the extra virgin olive oil in a stream so that you obtain a thick mayonnaise. Lastly, add the matcha and gently stir.

To avoid that the sprouts and flower petals for garnish become withered, keep them in the refrigerator wrapped in a paper towel dampened with water so that they stay full and crispy until the dish is eaten.

JERUSALEM ARTICHOKE CREAM WITH POWDERED GOLDEN YUNNAN TEA, LIQUORICE, GREEN OIL AND KAMUT CRISP

4 SERVINGS

FOR THE JERUSALEM ARTICHOKE CREAM
14 OZ (400 G) JERUSALEM ARTICHOKES
2 TSP (10 ML) EXTRA VIRGIN OLIVE OIL
1/8 OZ (6 G) SALT
APPROX. 3/4 CUP (200 ML) FRESH CREAM
3 TBSP (50 ML) WATER

FOR THE GREEN OIL FOR THE KAMUT CRISP
7 OZ (200 G) PARSLEY
1 CUP (250 ML) EXTRA VIRGIN OLIVE OIL
APPROX 1/2 CUP (50 G) KAMUT FLOUR
1 3/4 OZ (50 G) BUTTER
1 3/4 OZ (50 G) EGG WHITES
APPROX. 1/8 OZ (7 G) SALT
APPROX. 1/16 OZ (3 G) BERGAMOT WULONG POWDER
APPROX. 1/4 OZ (8 G) GRATED LIQUORICE ROOT
APPROX. 1/4 OZ (8 G) GROUND GOLDEN YUNNAN TEA
A FEW RADISH SPROUTS
A FEW EDIBLE GERBER DAISY PETALS

PREPARATION

To prepare the cream, peel and cut the Jerusalem artichokes into small chunks, then brown them in a pot on high heat with extra virgin olive oil for 2 minutes. Salt, then add the cream and water. Reduce the heat to low and braise for 20 minutes, covering the pot with a lid. When the artichokes are cooked, puree them with a hand blender until you obtain a thick cream. If it is too dense, add a bit of water.

For the green oil, blanch the parsley which you have previous stripped from the stem for 20 seconds, then cool in ice water. Drain and squeeze out the excess water and blend in a blender for 10 minutes with the extra virgin olive oil until you obtain a dark green oil. Pour the parsley oil through cheese cloth to filter the chlorophyll.

To prepare the crisp, stir together all of the ingredients until you have obtained a homogeneous mixture. Using a small spoon, transfer the mixture onto a sheet of baking paper and spread it into strips, then bake at a temperature of 355 °F (180 °C) for 6 minutes.

To assemble the dish, first lay down the cream, then the sprouts and flower petals (which should always one of the last elements of plating), the crisp, the liquorice and tea powders, and lastly, the green oil. As liquorice has a strong aftertaste, sprinkle it on the Jerusalem artichoke cream in moderation using your thumb and index finger to create a stripe over the mixture. Do the same with the Golden Yunnan powder.

HERB SALAD WITH EDIBLE FLOWERS AND BLACK PU'ER TEA RICE CHIPS

4 SERVINGS

FOR THE BLACK PU'ER TEA RICE CHIPS
8 3/4 OZ (250 G) CARNAROLI RICE
OLIVE OIL AS NEEDED
1/2 OZ (14 G) BLACK PU'ER TEA LEAVES
OIL FOR FRYING AS NEEDED.

FOR THE SALAD
1 SMALL HEAD OF LOLLO ROSSO LETTUCE
1 SMALL HEAD OF DELICATE CURLY GREEN LETTUCE
1 SMALL HEAD OF LATE-SEASON RADICCHIO
1 SMALL HEAD OF GREEN GENTILINA LETTUCE
1 SMALL HEAD OF ENDIVE
1 HEAD OF ESCAROLE
CHERVIL AS NEEDED
SOME RED RADISH, DAIKON, SUNFLOWER, ONION, AND GREEN SHISO SPROUTS
SOME ROSE, VIOLET, AND EDIBLE GERBER DAISY PETALS

To prepare the chips, toast the rice with a bit of olive oil until the kernels are well toasted and hot, then add enough slightly salted water to cover completely. Let it overcook, proceeding as you would for a risotto. Ten minutes before the rice is cooked, add the black Pu'er tea, and then finish cooking. The risotto must cook for around 40 minutes and be sufficiently creamy and thick. Be careful that it is not too wet. Then blend the rice in a food processor until it is creamy and smooth, free of lumps. Spread the mixture that you have made on a silicone baking mat, creating strips that are well separated and not too thin. Let them dry thoroughly until they are crunchy, then let them puff up for a few moments in the heated frying oil and drain immediately.

Prepare the salad by combining all of the ingredients. It is important to dress the salad at the last moment so that it is crunchy, tossing it gently so as to not damage the leaves and then let them gently fall onto the plate so that they remain fluffy.

STEAMED VEGETABLES WITH JASMINE SCENTED GREEN TEA POTATO CREAM

4 SERVINGS

FOR THE VEGETABLES

16 SMALL PINK TURNIPS
8 LEAVES TUSCAN CABBAGE
1 HEAD LATE-SEASON RADICCHIO, DIVIDED IN 4
1 HEAD ENDIVE, DIVIDED IN 4
1 SMALL HEAD OF CHARD
8 SMALL BUNCHES OF SPINACH
4 RADISHES
4 LEAVES OF SAVOY CABBAGE
EXTRA VIRGIN OLIVE OIL AS NEEDED
SALT AS NEEDED TO SALT THE VEGETABLES AFTER COOKING

FOR THE POTATO CREAM

1 LB 2 OZ (500 G) POTATOES
1 1/4 CUP (350 ML) FRESH CREAM
APPROX 1/8 OZ (6 G) SALT
1/2 OZ (16 G) JASMINE PEARL TEA

PREPARATION

Clean and cut the vegetables, then steam them separately. After cooking each of them for several minutes, arrange them on a tray covered in paper towels to eliminate any excess water. Dress with extra virgin olive oil and salt.

To prepare the cream, boil the potatoes in a tall sauce pan for 45 minutes, then peel and place in a blender and add the cream, salt, and Jasmine Pearl tea. Blend for a few minutes until the tea has released its full flavor.

When plating, lay the cream down first by spreading it using a serving spoon to form stripes, on top of which you will arrange the blanched vegetables. It is important that you dress them well with extra virgin olive oil so that they are more appetizing and glossy.

RICOTTA, SHRIMP AND BERGAMOT TEA

4 SERVINGS

8 FRESH SHRIMP
1/2 OZ (15 G) BERGAMOT WULONG TEA
1 2/3 CUP (400 ML) WATER
14 OZ (400 G) FRESH COW'S MILK RICOTTA
APPROX. 1/8 OZ (6 G) TAPIOCA FLOUR

FOR PLATING
A FEW PEA AND DAIKON SPROUTS
CHERVIL AS NEEDED
A FEW YELLOW VIOLET PETALS

PREPARATION

Shell the shrimp and freeze them for 12 hours: they must be very fresh, possibly still alive. Prepare the Bergamot Wulong tea infusion using 1 2/3 cup (400 ml) water and 1/4 oz (10 grams) of tea. The other 1/8 oz (5 grams) will be ground and set aside in a small bowl. Stir the ricotta and flavor it with 2 tbsp (40 ml) of the infusion and the remaining 1/8 oz (5 grams) of powdered tea. Cook the defrosted shrimp in the tea at a temperature of 80 °C (175 °F) for 2 minutes.
Boil the leftover tea for 10 minutes with the tapioca flour so that it reduces and condenses.

At this point, proceed to plating: dot the ricotta on a soup plate, next adding the tea reduction, which has thickened and cooled, then the shrimp, and finally the chervil, flower petals, and sprouts.

WULONG SHUI XIAN RAVIOLI WITH RADISHES, TURNIP GREENS, AND BEET POWDER

4 SERVINGS

FOR THE PASTA
APPROX. 2 1/2 CUPS (300 G) TYPE 0 FLOUR
APPROX. 1 1/2 CUP (200 G) SEMOLINA FLOUR
APPROX. 12 1/2 OZ (375 G) EGG YOLKS

FOR THE WULONG SHUI XIAN RAVIOLI FILLING
14 OZ (400 G) RICOTTA
APPROX. 1/4 OZ (12 G) WULONG SHUI XIAN TEA, GROUND WELL
APPROX. 1/16 OZ (3 G) SALT
1/16 OZ (2 G) FRESHLY GROUND BLACK PEPPER

FOR THE SAUCE
1 1/3 LBS (600 G) SMALL LEAF TURNIP GREENS
8 GREEN LEAF RADISHES
1/4 OZ (10 G) WULONG SHUI XIAN TEA POWDER
3 1/2 OZ (100 G) BUTTER

PREPARATION

For the pasta, stir the flours together well and add the egg yolks, continuing to work the dough until it is uniform and dense.

Season the ricotta for the filling with the Wulong Shui Xian tea powder along with salt and pepper.

To prepare the ravioli, roll the pasta dough out with a rolling pin until it is around 1 millimeter thick. Then cut the dough into 2 x 2 inch (5 x 5 cm) squares and place some filling in the center of each square. Fold each square over itself, creating a triangle and sealing it in order to obtain the classic ravioli shape.

Clean the turnip greens and radishes. Cook them in salted water for no more than 2 minutes. Melt the butter, then sprinkle the ravioli with the Wulong Shui Xian powder and add some melted butter to increase the flavor. Add the ravioli, the turnip greens, and the radishes into the melted butter off the heat, then proceed to plating in a large soup plate.

TEA TIME AND SERVING SUGGESTIONS

JAPANESE GENMAICHA TEA SOUP WITH VEGETABLES, SPROUTS, AND FLOWER PETALS

4 SERVINGS

FOR THE SOUP

APPROX. 3 1/2 CUPS (800 ML) WATER
APPROX. 3/4 OZ (22 G) GENMAICHA TEA
8 BABY CARROTS, GREENS LEFT ON
8 PURPLE TURNIPS
3 1/2 OZ (100 G) CELERY
8 SMALL FENNEL BULBS
5 OZ (150 G) SAVOY CABBAGE
APPROX. 1/4 OZ (8 G) SALT

FOR PLATING

8 3/4 OZ (250 G) WHEAT SPROUTS
A FEW RED ROSE PETALS
A FEW GARLIC AND SUNFLOWER SPROUTS
2 1/2 OZ (70 G) PEA SPROUTS

PREPARATION

Prepare a Genmaicha infusion with the amount of water and tea indicated. After 5 minutes, filter it through a fine mesh sieve.

Clean the baby carrots, turnips, celery, fennel, and cabbage. Chop the vegetables into similar sized pieces and boil for 2 minutes in salted water.

Once this is done, pour the Genmaicha infusion into a soup plate and add the vegetables. Lastly, combine the wheat sprouts, flower petals, and the other sprouts. To keep the vegetables and sprouts at their crunchiest, quickly assemble all of the elements on the plate and serve the soup very hot.

SENCHA AND RED RADISH SPROUT RISOTTO

4 SERVINGS

APPROX. 2 TBSP (25 ML) EXTRA VIRGIN OLIVE OIL
12 1/2 OZ (350 G) VIALONE NANO RICE
APPROX. 1/2 CUP (100 ML) WHITE WINE
1/4 OZ (10.5 G) SENCHA TEA
1 OZ (30 G) BUTTER FOR MOUNTING THE RISOTTO
APPROX. 3 TBSP (50 ML) EXTRA VIRGIN OLIVE OIL
FOR MOUNTING THE RISOTTO
SALT AS NEEDED
A FEW RED RADISH SPROUTS

PREPARATION

Bring a large quantity of salted water to a boil, which will be added to the rice to absorb. In a large saucepan, add the extra virgin olive oil and toast the rice, salting it slightly, until the kernels are searing hot. Add the white wine and let it simmer. When it has completely evaporated, start adding the salted water, then add the Sencha tea and continue cooking over high heat for 12 minutes.

At the end, the rice should be almost dry. At this point, add the butter and the extra virgin olive oil, add a ladle of the cooking water for the rice and beat the risotto hard in the pan so that all of the starches in the rice are released. Adjust the salt and serve on a plate. When it is ready to serve, let the radish sprouts fall lightly over the risotto so that they do not cook due to the heat.

LAPSANG SOUCHONG SPAGHETTI CARBONARA

4 SERVINGS

FOR THE SPAGHETTI

1 OZ (30 G) LAPSANG SOUCHONG
3 1/2 CUPS (600 G) SEMOLINA FLOUR
3/4 CUP (160 ML) WATER
7 OZ (200 G) EGG YOLKS
3 1/3 CUPS (300 G) PARMIGIANO REGGIANO CHEESE
1/2 OZ (15 G) FRESHLY GROUND BLACK PEPPER
APPROX. 1/4 OZ (8 G) SALT
4 CUPS (1 L) CREAM
POWDERED LAPSANG SOUCHONG AS NEEDED

PREPARATION

Grind the Lapsang Souchong tea and mix is with the semolina flour. Mix until the semolina flour is evenly speckled with black, then add the water and mix for 5 minutes. The dough should be very floury and grainy. Pass the dough through an extruder with a 0.01 (2 mm) bronze die, then place the spaghetti that you have obtained in the refrigerator on a steel cookie sheet on top of a paper towel.

In the meantime, mix the egg yolks, the Parmigiano Reggiano, the salt and the pepper in a steel bowl. Place this mixture in a double boiler and add the cream. Bring the mixture up to a temperature of 180° F (82 °C), continuously beating with a whisk to prevent the egg yolks from becoming lumpy.

Boil plenty of salted water for the spaghetti, then cook for 2 minutes over high heat and drain. Mix with the Parmigiano Reggiano cream away from the heat. Serve by sprinkling with a dash of powdered Lapsang Souchong.

FONDUE-STUFFED POTATO GNOCCHI IN BLACK DARJEELING TEA BROTH

4 SERVINGS

FOR THE FONDUE

7 OZ (200 G) FONTINA
3 EGG YOLKS
1 CUP (250 ML) WHOLE MILK

FOR THE BLACK DARJEELING TEA BROTH

3/4 OZ (20 G) DARJEELING CASTLETON TEA
2 CUPS (500 ML) WATER

FOR THE GNOCCHI

4 1/2 LB (2 KG) YELLOW POTATOES
4 EGG YOLKS
APPROX. 3/4 CUP (70 G) PARMIGIANO REGGIANO CHEESE, GRATED
1/4 OZ (9 G) SALT
APPROX. 2 1/2 CUPS (300 G) TYPE 0 FLOUR

FOR PLATING

A FEW DAIKON SPROUTS

PREPARATION

Cut the fontina into pieces and place in a double boiler, then add the egg yolks and milk. Bring the mixture up to a temperature of 175° F (80 °C), then mix with a hand blender and use it to fill a pastry bag. Refrigerate for about 2 hours.

Cook the potatoes in salted water for around 45 minutes, peel and mash them with a potato masher on a wooden cutting board, then let cool. Add the egg yolks, Parmigiano Reggiano, salt and flour. Knead quickly, without spending too much time on the dough (the more you knead it, the softer it will become). Stretch the dough between two sheets of baking paper at a maximum width of a quarter of an inch (0.5 cm), then cut the dough into squares of around 1.5 inches (4 cm) per side. Fill the center of each square with the fondue and then seal it as you would a dumpling.

Lastly, prepare the black Darjeeling tea broth by placing the indicated amount of tea to infuse in the water for 5 minutes, and then straining it through a fine mesh sieve.
Cook the gnocchi for 2-3 minutes, then serve in a soup plate where you have already poured some of the hot Darjeeling broth. Finally, garnish with daikon sprouts and serve.

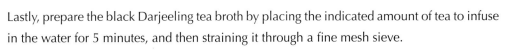

WULONG DONG DING LAMB WITH JERUSALEM ARTICHOKE CREAM

4 SERVINGS

FOR THE WULONG DONG DING TEA REDUCTION
1/2 OZ (14 G) WULONG DONG DING TEA
APPROX. 3/4 CUP (200 ML) WATER
APPROX. 1/4 OZ (8 G) TAPIOCA FLOUR

FOR THE LAMB
2 SMALL RACKS OF LAMB, AROUND 12 1/2 OZ (350 G EACH)
EXTRA VIRGIN OLIVE OIL AS NEEDED
BUTTER AS NEEDED
SAGE, ROSEMARY, AND BAY LEAF AS NEEDED

FOR THE VEGETABLES
4 SMALL HEADS OF CHARD
4 BABY FENNEL BULBS
EXTRA VIRGIN OLIVE OIL AS NEEDED
SALT AS NEEDED

FOR THE JERUSALEM ARTICHOKE CREAM
2 1/4 LB (1 KG) JERUSALEM ARTICHOKES
1 1/2 CUP (400 ML) FRESH CREAM

FOR PLATING
POWDERED WULONG DONG DING TEA AS NEEDED

PREPARATION

Prepare an infusion of Wulong Dong Ding, steeping the indicated amount of tea in water for 4 minutes, then filtering through a fine mesh sieve. Add the tapioca flour and reduce for 20 minutes over very low heat. Fill a pastry bag with the reduction and let cool for at least 4 hours

Prepare the lamb by trimming any excess fat, then browning in a nonstick pan with a bit of extra virgin olive oil, letting all sides brown. Add the butter and spices and reduce the flame to low, and with the help of a spoon continue to baste with the hot butter until cooked and pink in the center. Cut between the ribs to separate them and let the meat rest for a few minutes so that it loses any excess blood.

Boil the chard and the baby fennel, and garnish with a bit of olive oil and salt.
Arrange a few drops of the tea reduction on the serving plate, and place the lamb, the chard, and the fennel on top. Sprinkle with a bit of Wulong Dong Ding tea and serve.

LONG JING POACHED PRAWNS WITH CRUNCHY VEGETABLES

4 SERVINGS

FOR THE VEGETABLES
3 ZUCCHINI
3 CARROTS
4 BABY FENNELS
2 CELERY STALKS

FOR THE PRAWNS
APPROX. 1/4 OZ (12 G) LONG JING TEA
APPROX. 1 13/4 CUP (400 ML) WATER
8 PRAWNS

FOR PLATING
CHERVIL AS NEEDED
A FEW PEA AND GREEN SHISO SPROUTS
A FEW EDIBLE GERBER DAISY PETALS
A FEW LONG JING TEA LEAVES

PREPARATION

Clean and wash the vegetables. Remove the white part of the zucchini, cutting them into four pieces lengthwise and then into small pieces on the diagonal. Cut the carrots and celery in the same way. Sauté the vegetables over high heat in a nonstick pan, then add a ladleful of water and let it evaporate.

In the meantime, prepare the tea infusion and let it steep for 3 minutes. Filter once it is off the heat, and then immerse the previously shelled prawns in the tea for 4 minutes so that the flesh is tender and not affected by boiling.

Serve the prawns on a plate with the crunchy vegetables, the chervil, sprouts, flower petals, and a few Long Jing leaves.

TEA TIME AND SERVING SUGGESTIONS

LEG OF GUINEA FOWL WITH CARROT PUREE AND MOROCCAN MINT TEA

4 SERVINGS

FOR THE LEG OF GUINEA FOWL
1 3/4 OZ (50 G) CELERY
1 3/4 OZ (50 G) CARROTS
1 3/4 OZ (50 G) ONION
4 LEGS OF GUINEA FOWL
OIL, AS NEEDED
2/3 CUP (150 ML) WHITE WINE
1/4 OZ (10 G) TOMATO PASTE
SALT AND PEPPER AS NEEDED

FOR THE CARROT PUREE
14 OZ (400 G) CARROTS
APPROX. 1/2 CUP (100 ML)
EXTRA VIRGIN OLIVE OIL
SALT AS NEEDED

FOR THE MOROCCAN TEA REDUCTION
APPROX. 1/4 OZ (8 G) MINT GREEN TEA
APPROX. 3/4 CUP (200 ML) WATER
APPROX. 1/4 OZ (8 G) CASSAVA FLOUR

FOR PLATING
14 OZ (400 G) SPINACH LEAVES
A FEW FRESH MINT LEAVES
SALT AS NEEDED

PREPARATION

Dice the celery, carrot, and onion into small pieces then brown well with a bit of salt. In the meantime, brown the guinea fowl on each side in a nonstick pan with a bit of olive oil until it is dark brown in color, then add the white wine and simmer until boiling. Add the tomato paste and pour all of this in with the mirepoix of celery, carrots, and onion. Cook for around half an hour and a half, adjusting the water if necessary and seasoning with salt and pepper. While the guinea fowl cooks, prepare the puree: peel and clean the carrots, then cut them into small pieces. Brown in a bit of extra virgin olive oil and salt, then cover with a bit of water. Cook until the liquid is almost reduced by half, then blend with a beater, adding a bit more extra virgin olive oil and salt while mixing.

Prepare the Moroccan tea, let it cool and filter, then add the cassava flour and reduce over very low heat until the infusion acquires a gelatinous consistency.

Blanch some of the spinach for a few minutes in plenty of salted water, but do not let it boil too much, otherwise the color and consistency of spinach can become ruined from over cooking.

Once the hour and a half cooking time for the guinea fowl has elapsed, check that the meat is fully cooked and serve with the carrot puree, Moroccan tea reduction, spinach, a few fresh mint leaves, and the guinea fowl cooking juices, filtered and reduced by boiling into a dense and flavorful gravy.

BATTERED FRIED SMELTS WITH SPROUTS AND OSMANTHUS WULONG REDUCTION

4 SERVINGS

1 1/3 LBS (600 G) SMELTS

FOR THE BATTER

3 1/2 OZ (100 G) CORN STARCH
APPROX. 2 1/2 CUPS (300 G) TYPE 0 FLOUR
1/8 OZ (5 G) YEAST
APPROX. 3/4 CUP (200 ML) SPARKLING WATER
4 CUPS (1 L) VEGETABLE OIL FOR FRYING

FOR THE OSMANTHUS WULONG TEA INFUSION

3/4 OZ (20 G) OSMANTHUS WULONG TEA
APPROX. 3/4 CUP (200 ML) WATER
APPROX. 1/4 OZ (8 G) CASSAVA FLOUR

FOR PLATING

CHERVIL AS NEEDED
A FEW CURLY OR LETTUCE SPROUTS
A FEW VIOLET PETALS

PREPARATION

Mix the corn starch and the type 0 flour in a bowl. Add the yeast and the sparkling water and mix by hand until you obtain a soft and smooth batter. Place it in the coldest part of the fridge.

Put the frying oil in a suitable pan and bring to a temperature of 350° F (180 °C).
While the oil is heating, prepare the Osmanthus Wulong tea infusion, then add the cassava flour and bring to a gentle boil for around 25 minutes until the tea is thick. Cool and use to fill a pastry bag.

At this point, get the smelts and the frying batter. Dip the smelts one by one into the batter and fry them one at a time so that they do not stick together while cooking.

Place a few drops of the tea on the serving plate using the pastry bag, and place one fried fish on each drop of tea. Garnish with chervil, sprouts, and flower petals.

FRIED CHICKEN HEARTS WITH HUANG SHAN MAO FENG POACHED VEGETABLES AND BUCKWHEAT POLENTINA

4 SERVINGS

**FOR THE POLENTINA
(A THINNER VARIATION OF POLENTA)**

2 CUPS (500 ML) WATER

SALT AS NEEDED

7 OZ (200 G) "POLENTA TARAGNA" (FROM CORN AND BUCKWHEAT)

FOR THE VEGETABLES

14 OZ (400 G) CELERY

EXTRA VIRGIN OLIVE OIL AS NEEDED

SALT AS NEEDED

5 OZ (150 G) LATE-SEASON RADICCHIO

FOR THE CHICKEN

1 1/3 LBS (600 G) CHICKEN HEARTS

SALT, PEPPER, AND EXTRA VIRGIN OLIVE OIL AS NEEDED

FOR THE HUANG SHAN MAO FENG INFUSION

1/4 OZ (10 G) HUANG SHAN MAO FENG TEA

APPROX. 3/4 CUP (200 ML) WATER

PREPARATION

Boil the water in a small saucepan, lightly salting it, and sprinkle the polenta into the water, mixing constantly with a whisk. Cook for 45 minutes.

In the meantime, clean and wash the celery, then cut it diagonally into diamonds that are slightly less than one inch in diameter. Quickly sauté them in a bit of extra virgin olive oil, add salt, and then let them sizzle for around a minute. Add a bit of water to help the cooking

Clean and wash the radicchio, keeping only the ends of the innermost leaves.
Salt and pepper the chicken hearts and brown them in extra virgin olive oil over high heat, letting them color until dark brown, then add the Huang Shan Mao Feng and let simmer and reduce. Reduce the sauce until it is thick, glossy, and dense.
Assemble everything on a serving plate and serve.

MATCHA TIRAMISU

4 SERVINGS

FOR THE SAVOIARDI COOKIES (LADYFINGERS)
4 EGGS
1 1/4 CUP (250 G) SUGAR
2 1/4 CUPS (280 G) TYPE 00 FLOUR
GRATED LEMON ZEST AS NEEDED

FOR SOAKING THE COOKIES
1 2/3 CUP (400 ML) WATER
14 OZ (400 G) SUGAR
APPROX. 3/4 OZ (18 G) POWDERED BANCHA TEA
1/8 OZ (5 G) WILDFLOWER HONEY

FOR THE MASCARPONE CREAM
1 CUP (200 G) SUGAR
8 EGG YOLKS
14 OZ (400 G) MASCARPONE CHEESE
3/4 OZ (20 G) MATCHA POWDER
7 OZ (200 G) LIGHTLY WHIPPED CREAM

PREPARATION

To prepare the cookies, beat the eggs with the sugar for 25 minutes with an electric mixer. When the mixture appears whipped and quite solid, sprinkle in the flour, folding very delicately with a spatula from bottom to top to prevent lumps from forming, then add a bit of grated lemon zest. Pour the mixture into a nonstick baking pan lined with paper and bake for 25 minutes at 350° F (175 °C). When finished, wait a few minutes for the mixture to cool, then cut into uniform rectangles around 1 x 3 inches (2 x 6 cm) in size.
Preparate la bagna miscelando tutti gli ingredienti, inzuppatevi velocemente i savoiardi e disponeteli nella teglia in uno strato ben compatto e omogeneo.

Prepare the liquid to dip the cookies by mixing all of the ingredients together, then quickly dip the cookies and arranging them into a tight and uniform layer in a baking pan.
In the meantime, for the cream beat the sugar with the egg yolks until the mixture has puffed up, light and perfectly whipped. Add the mascarpone a little at a time, having previously whisked it, the matcha powder, and lastly the lightly whipped cream, which you will finish whipping when you incorporate it into the mixture. Cut the savoiardi in the pan using a cookie cutter, and arrange the shaped pieces on plates. Finish the dessert by covering with the mascarpone cream.

YOGURT BAVARIAN CREAM WITH VANILLA AND GREEN LYCHEE TEA SAUCE

4 SERVINGS

FOR THE CREAM
APPROX. 3/4 CUP (200 ML) WATER
1/2 CUP (100 G) SUGAR
1/4 OZ (10 G) GELATIN
JUICE OF HALF A LEMON
1 CUP (250 G) YOGURT
APPROX. 3/4 CUP (200 ML) FRESH WHIPPING CREAM

FOR THE VANILLA AND GREEN LYCHEE TEA SAUCE
5 EGG YOLKS
1/4 CUP (50 G) SUGAR
1/8 OZ (5 G) VANILLA ESSENCE
2 CUPS (500 ML) MILK
3/4 OZ (20 G) GROUND GREEN LYCHEE TEA

FOR PLATING
CHERVIL AS NEEDED
A FEW RED ROSE PETALS
A FEW MINT SPROUTS

PREPARATION

For the Bavarian cream, boil the water and sugar, then add and melt the gelatin, which you have previously softened for a few minutes in cold water and squeezed out any excess water, when removed from the heat. Mix well so that no solid residue of the gelatin remains. Add the lemon juice and yogurt, careful that the water, sugar, and gelatin syrup is not boiling, but is instead at room temperature. Then whip the cream and combine the two mixtures until you have obtained a smooth and well blended cream. Pour the mixture into your molds of choice and place them in the refrigerator for at least 4 hours.

To prepare the sauce, blend the egg yolks, sugar, and vanilla well. Boil the milk, flavoring it with the Green Lychee tea powder, then add the egg and sugar mixture a little at a time, continuing to stir. Cook the mixture over a double boiler, bringing it to a temperature of 180° F (82 °C), stirring continuously. Let cool quickly over water and ice, whisking continuously even after cooking to prevent lumps from forming.

Plate the desert, decorating with chervil, flower petals, and sprouts.

WHITE CHOCOLATE COULIS WITH BERGAMOT TEA AND VIOLETS

4 SERVINGS

FOR THE COULIS

1 LB 2 OZ (500 G) WHITE CHOCOLATE
1 1/4 CUP (350 ML) MILK
2 3/4 OZ (80 G) SUGAR

FOR THE BERGAMOT TEA INFUSION

1/2 OZ (15 G) GROUND BERGAMOT WULONG TEA
APPROX. 1/2 CUP (100 ML) WATER

FOR PLATING

A FEW EDIBLE RED AND YELLOW VIOLET PETALS
A FEW MINT SPROUTS

PREPARATION

Melt the chocolate in a double boiler with the milk and sugar, bringing the temperature up to 120° F (50 °C).

Prepare the Bergamot tea infusion and add it to the chocolate, filtering the mixture through a cloth.

Plate the chocolate coulis, and only then decorate with the flowers, mint sprouts and powdered Bergamot Wulong tea.

It is important that the coulis does not exceed 120° F (50 °C), as excessive heat may change the equilibrium of the chocolate.

72% DARK CHOCOLATE MOUSSE WITH BLACK SALT FLAKES AND MOROCCAN MINT TEA HONEY

4 SERVINGS

FOR THE MOUSSE

8 3/4 OZ (250 G) 72% DARK CHOCOLATE
APPROX. 1 CUP (180 G) SUGAR
APPROX. 1/2 CUP (100 ML) WATER
APPROX. 1/4 OZ (12 G) GELATIN
APPROX. 2 1/2 CUP (600 ML) WHIPPING CREAM

FOR PLATING

APPROX. 1/8 OZ (4 G) COARSE FLAKE SALT
A FEW VIOLET, RED ROSE, AND EDIBLE GERBER
DAISY PETALS
CHERVIL AS NEEDED
A FEW MINT SPROUTS

FOR THE MOROCCAN MINT TEA REDUCTION

APPROX. 3/4 CUP (200 ML) WATER
APPROX. 1/4 OZ (8 G) MINT GREEN TEA
1/8 OZ (5 G) GELATIN

PREPARATION

Melt the chocolate with the sugar in a double boiler along with the water and gelatin which you have previously softened in cold water and then squeezed out. Whip the cream and add it to the chocolate.

For the Moroccan mint tea reduction, boil the water and add the mint tea once the heat is off. Let steep for 6 minutes, the add the gelatin (previously softened in water and ice), and let solidify in the refrigerator for at least 3 hours. Using a pastry bag, decorate the plate with dots using the tea reduction before laying down the quenelles of chocolate mousse.

Let the mousse rest for at least 4 hours in the refrigerator. When it is quite cold, make four quenelles using a soup spoon and place one in the center of each plate, then arrange the flower petals as desired, along with the chervil and mint sprouts. Garnish with a few flakes of salt and serve.

WARM HAZELNUT MINI CAKES WITH HAZELNUT, AND GENMAICHA TEA CREAM

4 SERVINGS

FOR THE CAKES
7 EGGS
APPROX. 1 1/2 CUP (300 G) SUGAR
APPROX. 12 1/2 OZ (370 G) CHOPPED HAZELNUTS
APPROX. 1/4 OZ (8 G) GENMAICHA TEA
APPROX. 1/16 OZ (3 G) BAKING POWDER

FOR THE HAZELNUT CREAM
3 1/2 OZ (100 G) HAZELNUT PASTE
APPROX. 3 TBSP (50 ML) CREAM
1/4 CUP (50 G) SUGAR
1 OZ (30 G) CHOPPED HAZELNUTS

PREPARATION

To prepare the cakes, separate the egg yolks from the whites and beat the yolks with the sugar. Add the chopped hazelnuts and Genmaicha tea to the yolk and sugar mixture. Add the baking powder and then the whites, which have been beaten until stiff. Pour the mixture into individual greased molds and bake at 340° F (170 °C) for 25 minutes.

For the hazelnut cream, combine all of the ingredients in a steel bowl and cook in a double boiler, bringing the temperature to 150° F (65 °C) until all of the elements have thickened.

Here is a small tip to get the most intense flavor: serve the hazelnut cakes warm, if possible cooking them up to the last minute, so that all of the flavors can be clearly distinguished.

GLOSSARY

IN THIS SECTION WE WILL PROVIDE A BRIEF AND CONCISE GLOSSARY OF TERMS USED TO TASTE AND ASSESS THE QUALITY OF TEA. THIS LIST CLAIMS TO BE NEITHER COMPLETE NOR TECHNICALLY ACCURATE, PARTLY BECAUSE DIFFERENT CULTURES HAVE DEVELOPED DIFFERENT LEXICONS, AND PARTLY BECAUSE, WHILE THERE MAY BE A CERTAIN AMOUNT OF COMMON TERMINOLOGY, ESPECIALLY IN THE ENGLISH LANGUAGE, EVERY TEA TASTER AND EXPERT CAN CONTRIBUTE HIS OR HER OWN.
THE FOLLOWING OVERVIEW IS PROVIDED AS A GENERAL INTRODUCTION, IN ORDER TO IMPART SOME OF THE UNUSUAL AND LIVELY EXPRESSIONS CONNECTED WITH THE WORLD OF TEA.

COMMENTS ON THE APPEARANCE OF LEAVES

- *Body*: relates to the appearance of the leaves, which can be old or tender, light or heavy, and have a thick or thin flesh. Generally speaking, tender, thick and heavy leaves are best.
- *Clear tip*: the white down on the shoot is known as the "white tip;" if the shoot has several tips covered in thick down, these are defined as "clear tips;" the tips can be gold, silver or grey.
- *Dry*: dry tea leaves that have not yet been steeped.
- *Flawed leaf*: a badly cut leaf presenting rough edges on both sides of the cut.
- *Heaviness*: rolled leaves that are perceived as heavy in the hand.
- *Infusion*: steeped tea leaves removed from the water.
- *Powder*: the powder produced after rolling, generally associated with low quality tea and often used in tea bags.
- *Shoots*: tender tips, covered with white down, that have not grown into a full leaf.
- *Tender leaves*: tea consisting mainly of shoots with one or two leaves; these are round, narrow, thin, and with sharp pointy tips.
- *Uneven leaves*: leaves of uneven shape or thickness.
- *Well proportioned leaves*: leaves with a uniform shape, whether big or small, long or short, heavy or light.

COMMENTS ON THE COLOR OF LEAVES

- *Black-brown*: brownish black, with shades of grey.
- *Brilliant*: a leaf of a bright, vivid color.
- *Even*: a bright, homogeneous color.
- *Green-black*: a well-proportioned, velvety and even green, with shades of black.
- *Grass green*: pale green, indicating old or low quality leaves, or that the enzyme activity has not been successfully blocked.
- *Matt*: typical color of old, lusterless leaves.
- *Mixed*: leaves of an uneven color.
- *Rich green*: shiny jade green.
- *Rust*: dark matt red.

COMMENTS ON THE SCENT

- *Aroma*: the overall scent perceived indirectly in the mouth.
- *Bouquet*: the set of fragrances perceived in the nose.
- *Burnt:* the smell of burning caused by blocked enzyme activity or inappropriate heating or drying.
- *Delicate aroma*: elegant aroma in which no blend is perceived.
- *Elegant aroma*: graceful and elegant floral aroma, in which no one particular flower can be detected.
- *Grass aroma*: the scent of grass and leaves.
- *Pure and semi-sweet*: a pure, balanced aroma.
- *Sweet aroma*: aroma, similar to honey or syrup, reminiscent of lychees.
- *Toasted rice aroma*: similar to the smell of popcorn, typical of lightly toasted teas.
- *Vegetable aroma*: similar to the smell of freshly boiled cabbage; this term is often used to describe green tea.

COMMENTS ON THE COLOR OF THE LIQUOR

- *Brilliant:* clear, shiny liquid. Orange: yellow with a hint of red, just like the color of ripe oranges.
- *Brilliant green:* rich green with shades of yellow; clear and bright, this is the color of top quality green tea.
- *Cloudy:* unclear liquor with suspended substances.
- *Golden:* mainly yellow with shades of orange; light and brilliant, just like gold.
- *Green-yellow:* green with a hint of yellow.
- *Light yellow:* yellow and clear.
- *Orange-red:* dark yellow with shades of red.
- *Liquor:* in technical jargon, this is the liquid you drink, namely the tea itself.
- *Red:* overheated or old liquor, light or dark red in color.
- *Yellow-green:* yellow with a hint of green.

COMMENTS ON THE TASTE OF THE LIQUOR

- *Astringent:* dries the mouth due to non-oxidized polyphenols (typical of green tea) reacting with the proteins in the saliva.
- *Bitter:* an intense, bitter and sour aroma, that dulls the taste buds slightly.
- *Brisk:* a strong, invigorating and refreshing flavor.
- *Crude and sour:* an unripe, strong, sour flavor, usually due to insufficient withering.
- *Crude and tasteless:* insipid, tending towards bitter.
- *Fresh:* fresh and delicious, used to indicate slightly acidic tea that leaves a feeling of freshness in the mouth.
- *Full-bodied:* A strong, full-flavored infusion.
- *Generous:* ripe and dense; rich in flavor, without being cloyingly sweet.
- *Grassy and sour:* a strong, sour grassy taste.
- *Malty:* a flavor reminiscent of malt; this is an indication of good quality tea.
- *Metallic:* the unpleasant taste typical of badly withered tea.
- *Persistent:* leaves a lingering flavor in the mouth.
- *Pungent:* astringent without being bitter.
- *Pure and delicate:* ripe but not too dense.
- *Refined:* a subtle, sophisticated taste and aroma.
- *Rounded:* that fills the mouth with a feeling of fullness.
- *Semi-sweet:* a sweet but balanced aroma.
- *Smoked:* tea dried on smoky flames, providing a smoky aroma.
- *Strong:* a full, highly astringent taste, typical of a dark liquor.
- *Subtle:* a flavor marked by delicate yet complex aromas.
- *Sweet:* slightly sugary, not astringent.
- *Tannic:* the flavor of liquors rich in tannins, or polyphenols.
- *Tasteless or flat:* the thin, bodiless taste of humid tea.
- *Umami:* one of the five basic flavors perceived by the taste buds (the others are "sweet," "salty," "bitter" and "sour"); it is mostly used in Asian cuisine to describe the taste of glutamates, which can be detected in certain Japanese green teas.
- *Velvety:* a harmonious flavor reminiscent of the softness of silk and velvet.
- *Watery:* thin tea due to insufficient or inadequate infusion.

AUTHORS

FABIO PETRONI was born in Corinaldo (AN) in 1964. He currently lives and works in Milan. He studied photography and later collaborated with the most established professionals in the industry. His professional career soon led him to specialize in portrait and still-life photography, in which he has developed an intuitive and rigorous style. Over the years he has portrayed prominent figures of the Italian cultural, medical and economic scene. He works with leading advertising agencies and has devised numerous campaigns for prestigious businesses and companies known around the world. Moreover, he personally handles the image of major Italian brands. For White Star Publishers, he has published *Horses. Master portraits* (2010), *Mutt's Life!* (2011), *Cocktails, Roses* and *Supercats!* (2012), *Orchids* and *Chili Pepper: Moments of Spicy Passion* (2013). As the official photographer of the International Jumping Riders Club (IJRC), he handles the visual communication of equestrian competitions on an international scale.
www.fabiopetronistudio.com

GABRIELLA LOMBARDI was born in Alexandria in 1974. She lives and works in Milan. Her university studies led her to Granada, in southern Spain, where she breathed the air filled with Arab cultural influences, mixed with the aroma of the tea sipped in the many "teterias". It is here that she developed her passion for tea and all its rites. When she returned to Italy, she worked as a publicist for the most famous Italian agencies. Having given birth to two children, in 2010 she decided to change her life and realize her dream, opening the *Chà Tea Atelier*. This was the first shop in Milan with a tea room that specializes in the sale and tasting of prized teas. Ever an inquisitive globetrotter, she regularly travels to China in order to pick up the secrets behind the art of tea, honing her knowledge and skills, there where this extraordinary drink first originated. *Tea Sommelier* is his first book.

GIOVANNI RUGGIERI was born in Bethlehem in 1984, but grew up in Piedmont. He trained professionally in Michelin-starred Italian kitchens, such as Piazza Duomo in Alba and Scrigno del Duomo in Trento. Chef at the Refettorio Simplicitas, a restaurant of rigorous elegance in the heart of the Brera district of Milan, Ruggieri is committed to spreading a renewed approach to food, based on simplicity and with a strong emphasis on quality raw materials, selected according to their season and wholesomeness. Ruggieri serves authentic classic dishes and flavors, proposing many niche products typical of the local territory. His is a simple, sober, balanced cuisine, with a rustic, almost ascetic quality.

ALPHABETICAL INDEX OF TEAS

Assam Hatialli FTGFOP1 - SF, 161
Darjeeling Castleton ("Darjeeling Muscatel") - SF, 156, 212
Darjeeling Gopaldhara FTGFOP1 - FF, 157
Darjeeling Jungpana FTGFOP1 - Wonder Muscatel - SF, 158, 210
Darjeeling Margaret's Hope FTGFOP1 - FF, 159
Darjeeling Seeyok FTGFOP1 - FF, 160
Nuwara Eliya High Grown, 166
Ruhuna Golden Tips, 168-169
Uva High Grown, 171

Red teas, 23, 24, 26, 32, 55, 144, 145, 146, 147, 148, 149, 150, 151, 184, 193, 196, 210
Dian Hong, 147, 150, 151
Golden Yunnan, 150, 196
Lapsang Souchong - Zheng Shan Xiao Zhong, 147, 148, 210

Qimen ("Keemun"), 147, 149
Red Mao Feng, 151

White teas, 23, 24, 26, 32, 55, 117, 119, 120, 121, 122, 184, 193
Bai Hao Yin Zhen ("Silver Needle"), 120, 121
Bai Mu Dan ("White Peony"), 121
Ruhuna Silver Tips, 122

Yellow teas, 23, 24, 26, 32, 55, 109, 110, 113, 114-115, 184, 193, 232
Jun Shan Yin Zhen, 113
Meng Ding Huang Ya (Yellow Ya), 114-115, 232

ALPHABETICAL INDEX OF NAMES

ALPHABETICAL INDEX OF RECIPE INGREDIENTS

PHOTO CREDITS

All the photographs are by Fabio Petroni, except:
page 22 Mary Evans Picture Library
image of the Chinese character cha (meaning "tea") Joey Chung/iStockphoto

Gabriella Lombardi wishes to thank Chà Tea Atelier for supplying the tea and accessories;
Salvatore Nicchi, for his valuable advice on technical aspects;
Valentina Mecchia, for her infectious optimism;
Ettore, Elena and Emma, her life companions and greatest supporters.

Fabio Petroni wishes to thank Simone Bergamaschi, photo assistant;
Cristian Ginelli, art director;
High Tech Milano for the supply of accessories.

WHITE STAR PUBLISHERS

WS White Star Publishers® is a registered trademark
property of De Agostini Libri S.p.A.

© 2013 De Agostini Libri S.p.A.
Via G. da Verrazano, 15
28100 Novara, Italy
www.whitestar.it - www.deagostini.it

Translation and editing: Soget srl

ISBN 978-88-544-0767-1
1 2 3 4 5 6   17 16 15 14 13

Printed in China